More p

"*101 Tips for Telecommuters* is much, much more than the title imp... there are 101 extraordinarily valuable tips, and each one will significantly improve your effectiveness and efficiency. This is, however, not only a book for the increasing number of us who commute down the hall to our work space. It's really a field guide for all people who want to take control of their own lives, and work and live with a sense of mastery. *101 Tips for Telecommuters* will help you get your work organized, your life back, and it will make you and your employer (if it's other than you) very, very happy."

Jim Kc ... *ing the Heart*, and
Chairn

"*101 Tips fo* ... can be applied immediately ... ok is destined to become a ... mmuters, as well as for c ... vorkforce."
Richar... 9 Chair of the
Board ... STD)

"Whether y ... :w reality.
This book is ... th the telecommuters and ... from this
new way of ... of the issues
that a teleco ... of personal
productivity
Jac... enger Miller

"This book ... uting in its
proper role, ... e people,
and Debra L ... ctors of
telecommut
Connie

"This book i ... is so valuable
I have assign ... uters."
Dave E

"Very readal ... ld it to your
'must read' l ... king the
transition to
Steve M ... ince
Improv
Building Community: The Human Side of Work

"*101 Tips for Telecommuters* is an extremely valuable resource for anyone seeking to successfully telecommute or work effectively from a home office. Readers will learn how to plan for the most effective use of their workdays and to avoid pitfalls which can lead to failure. I highly recommend this book to anyone who is considering telecommuting, operating a home office or attempting to improve their efficiency."

Stephen M. Paskoff, President, Employment Learning Innovations, Inc.

"Telecommuting is hard work. This is the first practical set of advice for the new generation of distributed workers. Wonderfully, it addresses all aspects of surviving and thriving while working from home. A great read!"
    Elliott Masie, Editor of TechLearn Trends and President of The MASIE Center

"*101 Tips for Telecommuters* is the right book for those who want to telecommute rather than starting their own home-based business. Every company considering telecommuting should be passing out a copy of this book to each of their telecommuters."
    George M. Piskurich, Technology consultant and author of
    An Organizational Guide to Telecommuting

"Use this book to convince your boss that you can telecommute successfully—everything you need is here!"
    Deborah Dumaine, President, Better Communications and author of
    Vest Pocket Guide to Business Writing

"If I only had this guide when I opted to telecommute ten years ago! I learned by trial & error. This book covers it all, read it—overcome obstacles and reap the benefits!"
    Patricia Bruns, Senior Account Executive, Development Dimensions International

"Every telecommuter will gain tremendous insight from the author's first-hand experiences of living and managing the telecommuting process. Increased productivity, effective resource management, generating more income and understanding the key human factors for success will result."
    Jim Welch, Principal, Welch & Associates

"A practical and fun book. I found many ideas to use in my own work as a telecommuter. The style and content make it feel like a very helpful 'distance learning' experience."
    David M. Kolb, Senior Associate/National Accounts, Ridge Associates, Inc.

"A superbly practical guide to telecommuting resonating with the voice of experience. Some books explain what to do, others explain why to do it—Dinnocenzo's book does both. It's a goldmine of information with an application step for each tip, making it a must read if you want to telecommute or want to be a more effective telecommuter."
    Dr. Jim Dupree, Professor of Business and Communication, Grove City College

"Anyone who is considering working at home, either part time or full time, will find invaluable resources in this book. The telecommuter gets checklists and tips that lead to productive work from home, along with keys to avoiding pitfalls. As a human resource director, I can use this book to persuade our executives to support and encourage telecommuting."
    Dan Hupp, VP Human Resources, Blattner Brunner, Inc.

"An invaluable resource not only for telecommuters but also every manager who faces the decision of providing employees with the opportunity of 'working from home' some portion of their time. Debra's expertise in this subject matter becomes clear right from the start and her mindful approach of connecting tips and ideas to the practical business realities of telecommuting puts this book on my short-list of must read for managers."
    Richard V. Michaels, Managing Partner, Michaels McVinney, Inc.

101
TIPS
for
Telecommuters

Successfully Manage
Your Work, Team,
Technology
and Family

Debra A. Dinnocenzo

Berrett-Koehler Publishers
San Francisco

Berrett-Koehler Publishers, Inc.
450 Sansome Street, Suite 1200
San Francisco, CA 94111-3320
Tel: 415-288-0260   Fax: 415-362-2512
Website: www.bkconnection.com

Ordering Information

Individual sales. Berrett-Koehler publications are available through most bookstores. They can also be ordered direct from Berrett-Koehler Publishers by calling, toll-free; 800-929-2929; fax 802-864-7626.

Quantity sales. Special discounts are available on quantity purchases by corporations, associations, and others. For details, contact the "Special Sales Department" at the Berrett-Koehler address above.

Orders for college textbook/course adoption use. Please contact Berrett-Koehler Publishers toll-free; 800-929-2929; fax 802-864-7626.

Orders by U.S. trade bookstores and wholesalers. Please contact Publishers Group West, 1700 Fourth Street, Berkeley, CA 94710; 510-528-1444; 1-800-788-3123; fax 510-528-9555.

Printed in the United States of America

 Printed on acid-free and recycled paper that is composed of 85 percent recovered fiber, including 10 percent postconsumer waste.

Library of Congress Cataloging-in-Publication Data
Dinnocenzo, Debra A.
   101 tips for telecommuters : successfully manage your work, team, technology and family / Debra A. Dinnocenzo.
      p.   cm.
   Includes bibliographical references and index.
   ISBN 1–57675–069–8 (alk. paper)
   1. Telecommuting.   I. Title.   II. Title: One hundred and one tips for telecommuters.
HD2336.3D56   1999
331.25—dc21   99–35779
                                            CIP

First Edition

02 01 00 99   10 9 8 7 6 5 4 3 2 1

Designed by Detta Penna

Dedication

To my husband, Rick Swegan
*who cheerfully reviewed drafts
and provided helpful feedback,
while working overtime as
Mr. Mom/Head Chef*

And to my daughter, Jennimarie
*who consistently inquired
about the progress of my "story"
and volunteered to contribute the special foreword,
written on behalf of telecommuter children
everywhere*

Contents

Working Well with Your Family   65

Working Well with Your Team   *99*

Working Well with Your External Partners

Working Well with Tools and Technology *171*

Foreword

Telecommuting will be a major part of the 21st century's global environment. The workplace has been preparing for telecommuting for the past two decades. Emphases on employee empowerment, self-directed work teams, and techniques for improving productivity have been simultaneously preparing us to participate in a workplace exposed to continuous change. The landscape of business has moved from local to regional, from national to international, from multinational to transnational. In this age of the global community, telecommuting has made the transition from an exotic fad to a business imperative.

101 Tips for Telecommuters is a toolbox of practical ideas and solutions for both employees and employers who intend to succeed. Debra Dinnocenzo is not only a bright thinker who has great business savvy, she deliberately developed her career through a wide variety of business environments. Additionally, she is an applied researcher who recorded her experiences, pondered her observations, and learned from her results. She has captured her telecommuting experience and expertly packaged it into a book structured with great flexibility and containing a wealth of resources for people who want to work smartly from home.

The flexibility that is essential to your success as a telecommuter or telemanager has been carefully designed into this text, from first to last page. Unlike the flood of "how to" books currently filling bookstore shelves, *101 Tips for Telecommuters* demonstrates and models the traits so critical to telecommuting success. The versatile design accommodates your needs, whether you are an experienced telecommuter or are unsure of what telecommuting really means— and if it's appropriate for you.

This book will serve as an essential tool in helping you discover where to best begin your personalized journey into the world of telecommuting. Telecommuting opportunities exist in large and small organizations, for full- or part-time employees, as well as for nontraditional workers such as independent consultants, subcontractors, project managers, home-based businesses, and cottage industry enthusiasts. Workers who love to travel, as well as those who prefer to stay home in their cozy den, will find creative ideas, practical tools, shortcuts, time savers, productivity enhancers, well-thought-out business strategies and day-to-day common sense business advice. The bottom line is this: If you spend any amount of time working at home or think that you might, this book is for you.

Any organization looking to increase productivity, retain talented employees, and gain competitive advantage in the 21st century can't overlook telecommuting as part of its strategy. Those already implementing telecommuting should make this book required reading for their telecommuters and telemanagers. Those who are preparing to move into telecommuting won't want their people to be without this valuable resource to help "kick start" their telecommuting success.

As an 11-year veteran of telecommuting—for one of the largest distance education institutions of graduate degree programs in the world—I discovered that everything I needed as a telecommuter instructor and administrator over the years is conveniently presented in this book. Debra Dinnocenzo has done an insightful job of describing the world of telecommuting. If you currently telecommute or aspire to be a telecommuter, you won't find a more useful and experience-based resource for achieving great success with telecommuting. Further, not knowing how to telecommute effectively is sure to become a liability for anyone who wants to maintain his or her individual competitive advantage in the evolving workplace.

Ronald C. Fetzer, Ph.D.
Nova Southeastern University

Why It's Good to Work at Home

contributed by
Jennimarie Dinnocenzo Swegan
(age 5)

It's good to work at home because:

☺ All the kids get to spend more time with their families.

☺ The Moms and Dads don't have to drive as far to get to their offices. (In fact, they don't have to drive at all!)

☺ Moms and Dads don't have to have very many meetings and eat lunch at the same time.

☺ Dad has enough time to practice basketball with me.

☺ I get to meet Mom's work friends on the (videoconference) computer.

Preface

It's been difficult during recent years to avoid noticing the increased coverage that telecommuting has received in the business press. Stories about the challenges and rewards of telecommuting are especially visible during times of natural disasters (e.g., earthquakes, floods, blizzards) and other traffic traumas (e.g., bridge collapses, roadway reconstruction, the Olympics).

Much of the early coverage of the telecommuting trend focused on the increased availability of cost-effective computer and telephone systems. While these advances in technology have given us the proliferation of notebook computers, desktop videoconferencing, and vital levels of corporate computer network connectivity, we're beginning to understand the importance of the human side of telecommuting. *People* telecommute; computers and telephones are *tools* that facilitate the telecommuting process. As we look beyond modems and multimedia, a broad range of human factors impact the success of telecommuting. Understanding these human factors and learning how to effectively manage the nontechnical aspects of telecommuting, while competently handling the technical realm, is essential to your success as a telecommuter.

I envisioned this book as a succinct, easy-to-use guide for current and aspiring telecommuters. As a seasoned telecommuter, I've seen firsthand the factors that make telecommuting prosper or fail. I've also witnessed the significant impact telecommuting can have on one's quality of life—both good and bad. But from all that I've seen and experienced, I have found that telecommuting can have a predominantly positive impact on your quality of life, your productivity, your peace of mind, and (if you're like the rest of us) your eternal quest for the much-sought-after *balance* between work and the rest of your life.

All of the advantages, though, are contingent on your ability to telecommute *wisely*. In writing this book, my goal is to help you learn some of the secrets to effective telecommuting. It is my fervent hope that, in reading this book, you will discover ways to open doors to telecommuting success that enable you to prosper—both personally and professionally—by achieving whatever goals you have for your telecommuting venture. Until now, some of those goals were only dreams. With the right information, skills, and mindset, you can now transform those dreams into reality!

Debra A. Dinnocenzo
Pittsburgh, Pennsylvania, USA
1999

Acknowledgments

At the end of the long journey I've taken to complete this book, I'm left only with the final (and delightful) task of giving thanks. Naturally, there's a long list of people whose help made this a better book. More than that, however, was the unexpected reminder of just how wonderful people can be.

♥ Without the love and support (and occasional reminders to get some sleep) provided by my husband, Rick Swegan, frustration and exhaustion would have overtaken me long before the manuscript was completed. He and our daughter, Jennimarie, have been patient beyond reason and enthusiastic in spite of my all-too-frequent absences from them. I offer you both, the love and light of my life, my deepest thanks.

No one else cooked, ran errands, or brewed tea for me, but their help was, nonetheless, invaluable. My sincere thanks and appreciation to:

• Anne Palmer, who persisted in asking me, "How's that book coming along?" so many times that I finally decided to write it. Every author should be so fortunate to have a literary agent with Anne's energy, vision, determination, creativity, and skill.

• The team that comprises Berrett-Koehler Publishers, Inc., who saw the opportunity and voted to accept my book for publication. Special thanks to Steven Piersanti, for not tossing my proposal in the circular file; my editor, Valerie Barth, for her patience and guidance; and Pat Anderson, a kindred marketing soul whose insight and vision make all the difference.

• To my colleagues and friends, all of whom are *very* busy people, but who still made the time to help by reviewing my manuscript or offering their guidance, insights, or experience. Their collective feedback sharpened the focus of the book and added to the "real life" examples throughout. I'm amazed—and grateful—for the care they took and the detail they provided in their feedback. The book is what it is thanks to the help of: Lynn Arkan, Ray Bard, Terry Broomfield, Patricia Bruns, Bill Byham, Deborah Dumaine, Jim Dupree, Jody Ellis, John Hayden, Dan Hupp, David Kolb, Mark Little, Jerry Noack, Steve Pascoff, Alice Pescuric, George Piskurich, and Jim Welch.

- I owe a debt of gratitude (and I'm sure he'll collect!) to Ron Fetzer. His enthusiasm for the book was evident when he reviewed the manuscript and provided pages of ideas and suggestions, not only for this book but for the next one he's convinced I must write! Further, in spite of an impossible deadline, he agreed to provide the Foreword to the book and did miraculous work. Thanks, Ron, for your energy and vision.

- For every telecommuter, there's usually a boss who also believes in telecommuting or is willing to take the gamble to support an innovative way of working. Without the vision and support of three such leaders, I wouldn't have had the opportunity to acquire the experience I did as a telecommuter. I offer my sincere appreciation to Rich Wellins, J. Gordon Myers, and Dave Erdman. Without their support, so much would have been so unattainable.

How to Use This Book

101 Tips for Telecommuters is designed for current and prospective telecommuters or home-based workers who want to increase their level of skill and effectiveness. It provides information, suggestions, guidelines, insights and glimpses of reality from the "trenches of telecommuting" based on firsthand experience. With an emphasis on the relationships and interpersonal interactions critical to telecommuting success, this book offers readers a unique and practical view of the pros and cons, the good/bad/ugly, and the critical criteria for successfully and enjoyably working from home.

This book is focused primarily on the issues and needs of telecommuters—those who regularly work from home during some portion of their work week. However, many of the issues and challenges faced by telecommuters are strikingly similar to those of other home-based workers who may not refer to themselves as telecommuters. Therefore, others who work from home (e.g., consultants, salespeople, trainers, et al.) will find value for significant portions of their work-at-home needs and issues.

You can derive the greatest benefit from the book by selectively reading tips that align with your areas of greatest need, interest, frustration, or anxiety. While reading the book from cover to cover is an option, the book is designed so that tips can be read in any order. Refer to the next section, **Where to Begin**, for suggestions on the tips most appropriate for you as starting points.

TRANSFER IT PROMPTLY TO IMPROVE PERFORMANCE

- Each tip includes an addendum referred to as the TIP^2 which suggests you should "Transfer It Promptly To Improve Performance." Each TIP^2 offers action guidelines to help you apply the recommendations presented in the context of the tip.

- Reading the tips without taking the time to apply the TIP^2 to your work or your life will diminish the value of the tip and the book. Reading the tip and taking the action in the TIP² section will get you the best result.

- Therefore, I suggest that you read a tip each week or every few days, providing ample time to apply what you've learned or take the action steps suggested. This is far more critical than the specific order in which the tips are read, so prioritize them according to your needs. In this way, the information and action steps are relevant to you and to your specific needs as a telecommuter. This is a sure-fire way to ensure you're getting a great return on your investment of the money to purchase this book and your time to read and apply it.

Where to Begin

Relax! Unlike how so much of the rest of your life feels, it's okay **not** to digest this entire book **now** by reading it from cover to cover without a break. As a matter of fact, this is definitely not the way to derive the greatest benefit to you and your work (see the preceding section, **How to Use This Book**). To help you determine where it's best for you to begin, use the following guide. Prioritizing the tips and reading them according to your specific needs will provide more immediate and relevant results.

Statement most appropriate for you:	Begin with these tips:
I'm thinking about becoming a telecommuter.	1, 2, 12, 13, 26, 32, 33, 35, 36, 48, 68, 83, 85, 86, 88, 101
I want to telecommute and am ready to begin discussing this with my family and boss	1, 2, 3, 31, 35, 40, 48, 49, 61, 83, 85, 88, 101
I'm ready to start telecommuting, but need to plan/prepare my:	
• self	1, 2, 3, 4, 5, 6, 7, 13, 18, 19, 20, 21, 23, 24, 25, 26, 29, 30, 101
• office	1, 8, 10, 12, 13, 15, 16, 17, 86, 101
• work processes	1, 2, 3, 4, 5, 8, 9, 10, 11, 13, 15, 24, 25, 27, 101

- family   1, 2, 13, 31, 32, 33, 34, 35, 40, 42, 44, 46, 47, 101

- work relationships   1, 2, 3, 48, 49, 50, 51, 53, 56, 57, 58, 60, 61, 62, 63, 67, 68, 101

- equipment/supplies   1, 8, 9, 83, 84, 85, 86, 87, 88, 89, 92, 93, 99, 101

I've started telecommuting and on some days I think I've made a big mistake!

                                            1, 2, 3, 4, 6, 7, 11, 13, 19, 21, 24, 26, 29, 31, 32, 33, 40, 42, 48, 51, 56, 62, 66, 67, 84, 91, 94, 101

I've been telecommuting with some success, but I'm still encountering a few "bumps in the road" with regard to:

- family conflict/demands   31, 32, 33, 34, 35, 39, 40, 42, 47

- mixed signals or unclear expectations from my boss
                                              48, 49, 57, 58, 59, 61, 62, 63, 64

- uncooperative co-workers   48, 50, 51, 52, 53, 54, 56, 57, 58, 59, 60, 62, 63, 64, 65, 67

- distance communication/meetings
                                              48, 57, 58, 60, 62, 63, 64, 65

- priorities and productivity   2, 3, 4, 5, 7, 8, 9, 10, 11, 15, 16, 19, 21, 22, 23, 24, 25, 29, 61, 75

- disorganization and distractions 2, 3, 4, 5, 7, 8, 9, 10, 11, 15, 19, 21, 22, 24, 25, 33, 34, 61, 75

- loneliness   7, 23, 26, 30, 32, 48, 51, 54, 56, 57, 82

- overworking (again!)   2, 3, 4, 5, 6, 8, 9, 15, 21, 23, 24, 26, 29, 30, 32, 47, 56, 66, 68, 75, 91, 100

- unreliability of others   31, 32, 42, 45, 47, 48, 50, 51, 60, 62, 68, 71, 72, 73, 74, 78, 81

- technology snafus and crashes   17, 83, 84, 86, 91, 97, 99

Assess Yourself for Telecommuting Success

Telecommuting is not for everyone:
- You can get lonely and miss being with people every day.
- You may feel isolated and invisible.
- You might lose sight of goals and not feel motivated.
- You could detest some of the mundane aspects of working from home.
- You might experience more conflict with your family.

And it's not easy:
- You may find yourself working more hours than before you telecommuted.
- You could be frustrated by the hassles of technology when it fails.
- You can run into problems with co-workers who resent your telecommuting.
- You might experience breakdowns in communication with your boss or your team.
- You could find yourself spending more time than you imagined serving as your own maintenance person, computer technician, electrician, office designer, furniture mover, and filing clerk.

But the rewards are tremendous! As other telecommuters will tell you:
- "I'm so much more productive than when I commuted to the office everyday."
- "Now I can actually concentrate and think clearly without all the distractions and interruptions I used to deal with in the corporate office."
- "I love telecommuting . . . and my kids like having me closer to home. We see more of each other now, and that's worth any trade-offs that come with telecommuting."
- "It's helped me increase my output, be more responsive to customers, have more time for exercise, and eliminate much of the stress I felt from my long commute everyday."

You're certainly not alone if you find yourself wanting to telecommute or have already jumped on the telecommuting bandwagon. But before I learned how to telecommute successfully, I discovered that there are distinct skills, attitudes, and behaviors essential to that success. Many can be learned, developed, reinforced, and honed once you're aware of them and understand your own strengths and weaknesses with regard to the criteria for successful telecommuting.

Using this book as a guide will help you address many of the critical aspects of effective telecommuting. It's important, however, that you begin by identifying those areas that are of particular importance to you and your needs. By doing so, you'll gain greater insight to your own ability to succeed working from home and can focus your ongoing learning and development efforts to ensure your continued prosperity as a telecommuter.

TIP²

Use the following "Telecommuter Self-assessment Checklist" to identify areas of concern and strength for you as a telecommuter. To enhance the usefulness of this process, also give the checklist to:

- Your boss
- A trusted co-worker who knows you well
- Your spouse or significant other
- A close friend

Ask for their perspective on any obstacles to your success and compare their responses. Use the insight gained from the checklist to guide your decisions about whether, when, and how to use telecommuting to your best advantage.

TRANSFER IT PROMPTLY TO IMPROVE PERFORMANCE

Telecommuter Self-assessment Checklist

Put a check mark next to all those that apply to you. If you are thinking about becoming a telecommuter, consider whether items you *do not* check will create a barrier to your success as a telecommuter or will require extra effort on your part to overcome a potential obstacle.

If you are already telecommuting, use this checklist to identify any areas of difficulty that are detracting from your productivity or satisfaction as a telecommuter.

Personal Traits/Preferences

I believe I:

- ☐ enjoy working independently.
- ☐ like to think through and resolve problems myself.
- ☐ am a high initiative person.
- ☐ am not a procrastinator.
- ☐ can set and stick to a schedule.
- ☐ like to organize and plan.
- ☐ am a self-disciplined person.
- ☐ am able and willing to handle administrative tasks.
- ☐ can balance attention to major objectives and small details.
- ☐ do not need constant interaction with people.
- ☐ can work effectively with little or no feedback from others.
- ☐ enjoy being in my home.
- ☐ do not need frequent feedback or coaching.
- ☐ have the required level of verbal and written communication skills.
- ☐ can pace myself to avoid both overworking and wasting time.
- ☐ can resist a refrigerator that's only a few steps away.

Job Appropriateness

My job:

- ☐ requires minimal face-to-face interaction.
- ☐ involves many responsibilities that can be met by phone, fax, or modem.
- ☐ allows for accountabilities to be quantified, measured, and monitored.

☐ affords me the freedom to manage my work as I see best.

☐ does not require frequent interaction with work associates.

☐ involves co-workers who are supportive and collaborative.

Home Office Space/Environment

I have a space for my home office that:

☐ has an adequate amount of work space for my current needs.

☐ would provide opportunities for future expansion.

☐ has an adequate amount of storage space.

☐ has adequate lighting.

☐ has sufficient ventilation.

☐ has a safe number of electrical circuits.

☐ is quiet enough to allow me to concentrate.

☐ provides appropriate separation from home/family distractions.

☐ is a pleasant and comfortable space I'd enjoy working in.

☐ is a reasonable distance from needed business services.

☐ has no zoning or lease restrictions that preclude telecommuting.

☐ has adequate insurance coverage to protect business equipment.

Family Support

My family:

☐ is supportive of my desire to telecommute and will react positively.

☐ is willing to minimize distractions and interruptions.

☐ will not require care or involvement from me during work hours.

☐ can accept my need to focus on work during business hours.

☐ is stable and has no relationship conflicts that would be distracting.

Working Well in Your Home Office

2 Focus Your Life

Few things will undermine your telecommuting effectiveness as swiftly and significantly as a lack of focus. The myriad distractions that bombard a telecommuter (ringing phones, incoming faxes, buzzing doorbells, chatty friends, whining children, etc.) along with the ever-present demands of the moment (looming deadlines, crashing computers, demanding clients, frustrated co-workers, impatient bosses) contribute to our occasionally taking our "eye off the ball" with regard to our true focus.

A quick scan of the dictionary definition of *focus* produces words and phrases such as:

➡ *convergence*

➡ *adjustment*

➡ *positioning*

➡ *clear image*

➡ *central point*

➡ *sharpness*

➡ *concentrated*

Focus serves as:

◎ Your guiding light; the purpose underlying your actions.

◎ The vision to which you calibrate your achievements.

◎ The clear and unambiguous ultimate objectives or goals that justify your effort.

Achieving focus is at the core of success in nearly every enterprise. But a lack of it can be particularly detrimental to the telecommuter whose continued success is tied to achievement of results. While this is certainly true for focusing your job in general as well as the details of your daily work, it is also applicable to your overall life focus. The underlying reason for my foray into telecommuting is attributable to focus: the priorities in my life became clearer and my desire to telecommute evolved from those priorities. Once I embraced a vision of myself telecommuting, I moved toward opportunities and learnings that allowed my vision to transform—and I started telecommuting!

13

Somewhere there must be estimates of the huge amounts of money spent on goal setting, life planning, time management, and values-clarification systems and programs. Who wouldn't agree that having a life plan isn't a good idea? Who wouldn't agree that clarifying your values, establishing your life priorities, balancing your various life roles, etc. isn't essential to a well-lived life? But, how many of us actually do this type of life planning? And if we attempt it, do we have the discipline to follow through, refine, update, and implement our plan on an ongoing basis? Just how many (well-designed and well-intentioned) day planner/timer/runner systems have been abandoned and added to the accumulation of stuff we think there isn't enough time to do?!

Be careful not to let a time-consuming or misused planning system become a barrier to your life-planning efforts. So, abandon the system if necessary (or begin to use it properly), but don't abandon your focus! Without a clear definition of your life focus, your daily priorities and work goals soon become empty means to a dissatisfying end. Most important, like so much else in the life of a telecommuter, your commitment and discipline to use whatever process you choose is the real key to a focused life.

 TIP²

Schedule a life-focus planning session with and for yourself. Block off time on your calendar, and find an appropriate place where you can commit some undisturbed time to contemplate and create. In the spirit of simplicity, begin by defining the:

4 most important things in your life

3 most important values you hold

2 most important things you want to accomplish before leaving the planet

1 thing you want people to most remember about your life

Get more detailed if you want—write a life mission; identify your life roles and define the priorities in each role; write your eulogy; map out a 5-, 10-, and 20-year plan—but don't procrastinate on the major points until you have time for the detailed version. You'll soon figure out that the "big picture" represents the most critical aspects of your life focus; the details will fall into place naturally.

TRANSFER IT PROMPTLY TO IMPROVE PERFORMANCE

3   Focus Your Work

Bringing focus to your work is critical to defining your job purpose and accountabilities. As a telecommuter, with a strong orientation to achievement of results, clarity regarding your job and your accountabilities is a fundamental communication tool between you and your manager.

If you work remotely, be certain you clearly define your:

- Mission
- Job purpose
- Key measures
- Rewards

Your *mission* should relate to the mission of your organization and should express objectives in areas such as market share, growth, levels of service to customers, positioning of your business relative to the industry, and the competition or perceptions of the marketplace or your customer base. Your *job purpose* states why your particular position exists and how it supports the mission. For example, the corporate annual report might provide a clear mission. But if you think your job purpose is to expand marketplace awareness and your boss thinks you were hired to increase sales, it would be useful to sort this out sooner rather than later.

Specific *key results and measures* are absolutely critical. You and your manager must have a crystal-clear agreement on how your effectiveness and success will be measured. Without such performance measures, especially when you telecommute, there's a risk that evaluations of your performance will be based on subjective criteria or—even worse—on what's seen by your manager versus what you deliver in terms of results. Finally, *rewards* (merit increases, advancement benchmarks and timeframes, bonuses, other perks) should be clearly tied to performance measures. Otherwise, there's a huge risk of confusion, assumptions, second-guessing, disappointment, anger, resentment, and job dissatisfaction.

When you telecommute, it's essential that you take steps to clarify agreements between you and your manager to ensure that your job focus is clear. In my telecommuting work arrangements, I've consistently supplemented my telecommuting agreements with more specific job performance measures documented through the performance management process (Tip 61). However it is handled, *be sure* it's addressed. Take the initiative when necessary to discuss, clarify, and document the terms of your role and your relationship with whoever evaluates your performance and influences your future. Therefore, if your organization doesn't utilize a structured telecommuting agreement or performance management system, create one and negotiate the details with your boss.

Remember that ultimately *you* are responsible for managing your performance, your work, and your future (Tip 30) and for determining on a day-to-day basis how best to ensure that your goals are realized.

 TIP²

Create a job plan that includes the following items:

1 Purpose statement for your position with a clear statement of the added value you bring to:

   • Your organization

   • Customers

   • Other stakeholders

2 Identify at least five key results you're expected to achieve, with specific measures by which your results are made visible.

Discuss/review this with your manager and document your agreements.

TRANSFER IT PROMPTLY TO IMPROVE PERFORMANCE

Focus Your Day

Regardless of the goal setting or time management system you use when telecommuting, you should begin each day knowing:

- What your *priorities* are (and why they're critical).
- What you need to *accomplish* (be certain you can quantify, measure, or otherwise clearly define this).
- What your *game plan* is for achieving the needed results (this includes both the "how" and "when" components of your daily action plan).
- What the *rewards* are for accomplishing your goals for the day (the immediate payoffs to you personally and professionally).

Your daily *priorities* are based on your job focus (Tip 3) and are the "call to action" for your day. For example, your priorities may relate to things like closing sales, completing articles, or designing strategic change plans. What you need to *accomplish* on a given day would be more specific and clearly measurable: complete a sales proposal, finish another phase of research, or complete the development of a change-management survey. While clarifying priorities and tasks to be accomplished are important to anyone who values productivity, telecommuters can be especially vulnerable to factors that diminish daily focus. Aside from distractions and demands of the day, you must maintain your focus without the benefit of co-workers, team members, or other more traditional workplace influences that may contribute positively to focus. For example, if a team is pulling together a major presentation or finalizing a project design, the energy and visible signs of progress that may exist in a team work area or a project "war room" won't exist in your home office. Since you'll need to maintain the same focus, however, you'll also need to be clear about what must be done when you leave your office at the end of the day (hopefully, at a civilized hour!).

Your *game plan* includes a list of "to do" items that support the accomplishments you're targeting for the day. These items could involve anything from phone calls with clients, conference calls with team members who are collaborating with you on a project, documents you need to write, feedback to be reviewed and discussed with colleagues, meetings with your manager, etc. Your game plan would detail the importance of each task, when you need to complete it, and how. For example, a sales executive may note in her/his schedule for the day that one of the "must do" items in connection with a major proposal is the completion of the pricing plan, to be accomplished by calling the marketing manager for input on the discount schedule and reviewing the draft plan with the sales manager before 2:00 P.M. so it can be faxed to the client to meet the 4:00 P.M. deadline. Of course, the sales executive also would plan the reward for completing and faxing the proposal (and completing other work targeted for that day).

Rewards (Tip 29) can be anything that provide incentives and motivate you (take a snack break with the kids, head out to the gym, visit a favorite chat room on the Internet) and keeps you focused on the things that contribute to your success in your work and your effectiveness as a telecommuter. Specific daily goals and associated rewards were vital to my ability to complete this book. On a few days (or nights) when deadlines were approaching, my reward was fairly basic: complete the tips that had to be written for that day, *and then* I could leave the office and/or finally get some sleep!

 TIP²

Decide which daily planning process is best for you. If you're not sure, start, at a minimum, with a blank piece of paper (or a new document on your computer). Be sure to put in writing your prioritized "to do" items for your next work day. It's a simple step, but all the great journeys begin with one!

To get more specific, determine the:

4 top priorities in your current work.

3 specific accomplishments targeted for your next work day.

2 actions you must take to complete your accomplishments.

1 reward you'll attach to completion of targeted accomplishments.

TRANSFER IT PROMPTLY TO IMPROVE PERFORMANCE

5 Avoid Time Wasters

Being a advocate of telecommuting, you're likely to appreciate the value of time and ways to utilize it efficiently. It's likely you've already calculated the time you are or could be saving by telecommuting. Perhaps you've also identified all the things you can accomplish with the extra time telecommuting will provide. While thinking through all of this is helpful, beware of "activity creep"!

"Activity creep" is the slow emergence into your day of "stuff" that needs to get done but is not essential to achievement of your key daily goals. When you work in a traditional workplace, this "stuff" simply lingers in the back of your mind and is annoying. But when you telecommute from home, it's very much an "in your face" kind of annoyance that results in the waste of that precious time you so much wanted to save.

Here are just a few distracters that, in excess, may be a drain on your time and ability to achieve results:

- Reading the newspaper
- Playing computer games
- Exercising
- Visiting with neighbors
- Cleaning/light housekeeping
- Talking with family members
- Laundry
- Doing filing
- Running "quick" errands
- Organizing papers, files, drawers, closets, etc.
- Watching television
- Answering the door or home telephone
- Taking snack/refreshment breaks
- Talking on the telephone (personal chatting)
- Surfing the Internet
- Reading/filing personal mail

- Paying personal bills

Of course, some of these distracters may be on your list of fun things to do. Great! Use them as rewards or activities during work breaks (Tip 24). The easiest way to avoid time wasters is to be conscious of the ones that plague you. Make a commitment to yourself to use your time wisely and keep yourself focused each day (Tips 2, 3) on the essence of your work and your key accomplishments for achieving your goals. If the threat of failure isn't enough to motivate you, be sure to give yourself other rewards (Tip 29), incentives, or consequences that keep those time wasters at bay.

TIP²

- ⊕ Think about and list the major time wasters that create "activity creep" in your day.

- ⊕ Right now—make a commitment to yourself to eliminate (or better manage) two of them this week.

- ⊕ Make your commitment visible. For example, you could make a big sign or poster on which you write the time waster with a big red circle around it and red line through it. Or make little signs with a key word or symbol to remind you of a critical work goal (such as your sales goal for the month/quarter/year). Post your reminders near opportunities to waste time (on the file cabinet, refrigerator, pool table, telephone). The point is to ask yourself in the moment, "Is doing this activity right now the best use of my work time?"

T R A N S F E R   I T   P R O M P T L Y   T O   I M P R O V E   P E R F O R M A N C E

6 Maintain a Healthy Balance (Manage the Workaholic Within)

A great myth of telecommuting is the inherent—or automatic—attainment of balance. True, it's possible to rack up great savings in commute time which, in theory, can be redeployed as more time for family, recreating, relaxing . . . or more work! So, here's a simple rule of thumb: If you were a workaholic before telecommuting, you'll have a greater tendency to continue that pattern after telecommuting. The reasons for this are simple—you've only changed the location of work, you didn't get a frontal lobotomy! The situation is a bit like your computer, which, loaded with the same software, operates the same way in your home office as it does in your living room: same software, same hardware, same performance.

In many cases, this means setting reasonable limits to your work hours (except during peak times like end-of-month billing, getting a big proposal out the door, or responding to a client crisis). Otherwise—especially for the typical goal-oriented, high-initiative, hard-charging workaholic—you'll begin to feel as though you never really leave work. One of my telecommuter friends considers this to be the biggest obstacles he had to overcome—until he finally got his office out of a corner in his family room. Only then did he have a more tangible way to distance himself from work during nonwork hours and thus achieve some of the balance he needed. You, too, need to turn out lights, close doors, avoid checking e-mail or voice mail, let the answering machine respond to a call—in general, plan ways you will ensure that the balance you seek is indeed achieved.

If you were desperately seeking balance before telecommuting, you'll need to maintain the same—or stronger—commitment to achieving it as a telecommuter.

TIP²

▽ Visualize your ideally balanced life. Actually write out a daily schedule for your ideal day. Use a daily schedule format, a pie chart, or whatever tool helps you make your ideal plan specific and visible.

▽ How does it compare to ways you are currently investing your time and energy? (You may need to track your schedule for a few days to be more objective about how your time is spent.)

▽ Now find that prioritized plan for tomorrow and be sure that some of your vision for a balanced life is reflected in your plan.

Do *at least* one thing tomorrow that moves you toward the balance you're seeking.

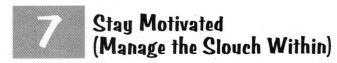

Stay Motivated (Manage the Slouch Within)

You're undoubtedly a highly motivated, high-achieving, self-starter type of person with unbounded confidence that you will achieve high levels of performance and output as a telecommuter. And when all the forces of the cosmos and the dynamics of your universe converge in perfect harmony, this is likely to be the case. But let's talk about reality. Those forces and dynamics don't just occur; you make them occur or respond to them in ways that keep you motivated, focused, and productive. How do you minimize factors that compromise your motivation and productivity?

An important key to staying motivated is to avoid procrastination. This is a particular challenge, even for highly motivated telecommuters, since many of the contributors to procrastination are ever-present in the telecommuting workplace (such as household chores, family distractions, personal tasks, television, exercise equipment, etc.). So, use these guideposts to maintain your motivation and keep the "slouch" at bay:

- Keep your focus (major goals, daily to-do tasks) in mind AND visible.

- Establish a system for tracking your accomplishments. Be sure it's easy to use (not another time-consuming excuse to avoid your real work!) AND visible. One telecommuter I know insists that he nurtures his sense of progress with a simple TO DO list. The important aspect of this for him is that he diligently crosses out each item as it's completed. Beyond the sense of achievement, it also serves as a method to track results. Other telecommuters use computer-based systems that accomplish the same objectives. (It's debatable, however, if one gains more satisfaction from vigorously crossing out an item on paper or hitting the delete button on the computer!)

- Organize your work into chunks that you can tackle in manageable pieces (remember that journey of a thousand miles and the one-step strategy).
- Set deadlines for accomplishing tasks.
- Do the hard stuff (probably also the important stuff) FIRST.
- Take breaks and/or switch activities periodically, using this technique as a way to either capitalize on your energy patterns or reward yourself for accomplishing a critical task. (Remember to limit your time commitment to reenergizing or rewarding activities. Too much of a good thing can be both wonderful and destructive to your best-laid work plans!)

Bottom line: Plan your work and work your plan—and do so relentlessly.

- Be sure you can answer "yes" to the following questions:
  - ✓ Do you have a workable, visible plan?
  - ✓ Is your tracking system functional and visible?
  - ✓ Do you know your priorities and have deadlines attached to action items?
- Make a list of at least 10 activities you can do or things you can give yourself when you need a short break or have earned a reward, especially in connection with accomplishing a task that was previously in your procrastination file!

TRANSFER IT PROMPTLY TO IMPROVE PERFORMANCE

Get and Keep Your Office Organized

Tom Peters has written eloquently about thriving on chaos, but it's an organizational state of mind—not the way you want to approach telecommuting. It's not even open for debate; it's a given, a truism, an unalterable fact of telecommuting life: lack of organization will doom you.

Managing the tons of paper (weren't we fantasizing about the paperless office just a decade ago?!) is inherent in your ability to be organized (Tip 9), and efficiently processing the mounds of mail you receive (Tip 11) is vital. But you need a context in which to manage the "stuff" of your day, and this context is created by systems and structure.

Unfortunately, you can't run to the local office superstore for your complete, customized system in a box! You need to create your own systems, based on your needs, priorities, type of work, and individual style. You can, of course, buy the components required to create workflow and organization systems that allow you to eliminate clutter on your desk; move essential work tools and resources under furniture, overhead, on the walls, onto shelves, into cabinets or lateral desktop files; or store items used less often in containers that provide easy access when you do need them.

Remember, this is nonnegotiable. It's essential that you analyze your work requirements and design systems that keep you organized. Does this mean you must have a clean desk when you leave your office each day? No, not necessarily. (Based on how my desk looks at the moment, I'm certainly relieved to know there are no hard and fast "clean desk" rules!) But if you continue to find yourself wasting precious time looking for things in all those stacks of paper, consider it a warning sign. Here's a good rule of thumb: If you spend more than 10 minutes every day looking for a file, your favorite scissors, a phone number, someone's business card, your supply of sticky notes, an old proposal, a purchase order, or anything critical to your work (and your efficiency), you need better systems.

If you're not good at creating systems, hate doing it, or don't think you have time, hire an organization consultant to do it for you. But only you can *keep* the system working well, so it's vital that you have systems tailored to your needs and style.

TIP²

Quickly scan your office and identify:

5 Things on your desk that you can relocate to a smarter place. (Now move them.)

4 Things in your closest desk drawer that aren't used frequently enough to keep them there. (Now find a new storage space for them.)

3 Files in your closest file drawer or desktop files that haven't been used in at least a month. (Now move them to a more appropriate file drawer or box.)

2 Areas where you have space that's not being utilized most effectively. (Now rearrange them.)

1 Thing you can buy that improves the organization of your office. (Add it now to your running list of things to order for delivery by your office supplier.)

TRANSFER IT PROMPTLY TO IMPROVE PERFORMANCE

9 Get and Keep Your Day Organized

Just as important as systems is the structure or routine of your day. Telecommuting has the appearance—and misconception—to others of being an unstructured, easy-going way of working. Successful telecommuting could not be further from this misperception.

Most successful telecommuters have a fairly structured routine they follow daily. This doesn't mean they overlook the need for flexibility, as with any typical workday. But, it's not a free-for-all in the way the day is approached—as much as possible there are set times for planning, phone work, project work, meetings, etc. And all of the daily activities of the successful telecommuter are based on and driven by priorities (remember focus!).

It is also essential to manage with a solid "calendaring" or scheduling system, along with a to-do list or tickler system that functions as a central input and output point for all of your tasks. This can be a pocket calendar, binder-based calendar, wall calendar, computer-based calendar and scheduler, notebook with prioritized action lists—whatever works well for you and your business. In spite of the best organized calendar and to-do list, you're still bound to have a cluttered mind, so it's important to avoid trusting any more to memory than necessary. Therefore, discipline yourself to write EVERYTHING down when you think of it—and then transfer it a.s.a.p. to your main scheduling system. Don't forget to be flexible when necessary—if you think great thoughts while exercising, keep a microcassette recorder handy. (I'm sure my neighbors are somewhat curious about what I'm saying into my recorder as I dictate along my power walk route!) Do the same in your car if you travel or commute periodically—talking is safer than writing while driving! And if solutions to the world's great problems come to you in the shower, install a writing board and grease pencil on your shower wall.

To get and stay organized, it's just as your mother always told you: a place for everything and everything in its place. This applies to all of your tools, resources, supplies information, AND events, tasks, commitments and other to-do items.

TIP²

✎ Confirm that you have paper and pen near every phone in your house, near your bed, in the bathroom, in your car, and anywhere else where you typically think of things that you need to do.

✎ Think about the other places where you want to capture your thoughts and create a way to do so even if the paper method won't work (microcassette recorder in your car, waterproof writing board for your shower, etc.).

✎ Get in the habit of gathering those notes and reminders so you can quickly integrate them into your central calendar and planning system.

10 Keep the "Administrivia" Under Control

The devil is in the details, as they say, but nowadays the more dangerous devil probably lurks in your data. More pointedly, anything that compromises your ability to manage, track, file, and retrieve information is a serious villain and a major threat to your success as a telecommuter. Therefore, you must be passionate about organizing the current and archived information relevant to your work.

Whether you do this electronically or with traditional paper files (and usually it's a combination of both), how you manage information greatly impacts your efficiency and, ultimately, your success. Don't go cheap here—invest in filing and/or data management systems that are first-rate. Buy good equipment—sturdy file cabinets and plenty of them, portable file bins (on wheels) for easy access to a current project or client files, a fabulous rolodex or a great business card scanning software package—whatever choices are most suited for your specific requirements.

Get help from a consultant that specializes in office organization or data management if you're not an organizational genius about such matters. But, once again, how you individually work with the system is essential to its success, so it must be customized to your needs and to the way you manage your work. A good consultant (e.g., one that will install a system that will work for you) will ask lots of questions about your work, what you do, how you do it, how you access information, your preferences, the things you hate, your needs, your limitations, your budget, and your time constraints. Your future needs should also be a consideration since your filing system should be designed to expand as your needs change and your archived data grow.

If you can't afford a consultant, consider bartering for the services (Tip 79). At the very least, attend a workshop or read a few books that focus on data organizing systems.

As for your tendencies to be a pack rat, there's no easier way to begin feeling that your work is taking over your entire house than to have file boxes stashed in corners and closets well beyond your office. One important rule: PITCH IT if you can. (Note: My husband assures me that I'm living proof that achieving perfection on this suggestion may be a fantasy!) Otherwise, a few hints:

- Keep current project or client files as close to your work space
  as possible, with other information (topical files, sales or marketing material, frequently used forms, etc.) kept at a reasonable
  distance from your desk.

- Keep noncurrent files that must be retained someplace other
  than your office, if possible (such as the basement, garage,
  closet). If these files require a significant amount of storage
  space, consider other options such as moving them to a corporate records retention facility or a local storage facility that provides a dry, climate-controlled, lighted indoor environment.

- Establish specific time frames for reviewing current files so they
  can be moved to storage as soon as possible; provide discard
  date on archived files so they'll automatically be destroyed when
  no longer needed.

One experienced telecommuter I know insisted that I include a
reminder about protecting yourself against the hazards of your files
being discarded without your consent. He discovered, with much
angst, that young grandchildren in your office apparently can identify and activate the delete key on the computer faster than you
might realize. So, while this minimizes your electronic storage demands, the judicious use of passwords might be advisable under
some circumstances!

TIP²

Maintain a master file list in your computer (print a hard copy
for backup) reflecting file name, contents, and location. Update it re-
ligiously whenever any file is moved or altered. The time investment
required to do this will pay off handsomely whenever you quickly
search your master list to locate a needed file.

TRANSFER IT PROMPTLY TO IMPROVE PERFORMANCE

11 Manage the Maddening Mounds of Mail

You may recall feeling burdened in the not-too-distant past by the volume of paper that filled your in-basket. It seemed that days would be filled with meetings, travel, and "normal" work, followed by the seemingly endless end-of-day processing of mail. (Unless, of course, you stuffed it in your *extra* brief case and took it all home to read!) Then the enlightened age of technology brought us the time-saving (and supposedly paperless) wonders of voice mail and e-mail . . . and you saved time, right? Not likely, since now you have three inbound sources of mail instead of one! And, no doubt, you feel as if you're drowning in it all. How can you stay afloat?

The overriding guide on handling mail is to do it as quickly as possible BEFORE it backs up badly. (The plumber can unclog your pipes, but only you can flush out the mail that awaits you.) I vividly recall times when I was locked in meetings for days or out of touch due to travel or had taken a few days of vacation only to face upon my return 147 e-mail messages, 63 voice mail messages, and a huge box of mail. You, too? Recall those times, remember the feelings of dread, and swear to yourself right now that you'll never let it happen again. But, how?

Processing your mail quickly doesn't mean you handle it as soon as it appears. Set aside specific times during the day to deal with all forms of mail. Overcome the temptation to read that fax when you hear the fax machine humming or switch to e-mail when your computer signals the arrival of a message. Don't worry—they'll still be there when it's time to read them! For all types of mail you receive, following these simple steps:

- Do an initial sort and quickly trash anything of no value. (Also delete from e-mail anything sent by an unknown addressee and avoid being on lists for automatic distribution of e-mail messages or new releases unless they're essential to your business.)

- Prioritize the items you're keeping into folders, boxes, files or piles: *Act Now, *Do Later, *Read, *File.

- Handle the *Act Now items immediately, remembering to be as brief as possible and respond to only those items that require a response. (Yes, your mother said to always say "Thank you," but she didn't realize that doing so would someday clutter someone's e-mail box!)

- Deal with the *Do Later and *Read items as time permits, always looking for creative uses of snippets of time (while on hold for a caller, during lunch, in the bathroom, etc.).

- Use drive time to keep on top of voice mail (following "safe cellular" guidelines, of course), and always leave your office with something from your *Read file should you encounter a delay or reading opportunity (when your vehicle is NOT in motion!).

TIP²

☞ Review your system for processing mail and your sorting system. If you don't have clearly designed places for different types and priorities of mail, set up the appropriate places now.

☞ Be sure that your *Read items are easily accessible near your office door (so you can grab them quickly on your way out when you may have opportunities to catch up on your reading backlog).

☞ Also, check the size of your trash can—you probably need to order a larger one.

TRANSFER IT PROMPTLY TO IMPROVE PERFORMANCE

12 Determine the Best Location for Your Home Office

Once you've decided to work from your home-based office, deciding where to locate your office in your home is a critical issue. (Actually, you should have given this some thought before pursuing the telecommuting option to ensure you indeed have appropriate space and work conditions essential to telecommuting success.) As you consider options within your home, there are a few factors to consider first:

- How much space will you need? (Base this on: the type of work you do; the furniture and equipment you'll require; the necessary access to supplies, files, and other materials; and the realization that you'll fill the space faster and need more of it than you expect.)

- What access will others need to have to your office? (Will you have meetings in your office? Will an assistant work with you?)

- How much psychological or symbolic distance will you need between your office and your family and your living space?

- How much physical separation will you need to give yourself to minimize the distractions presented by your family and the rest of your home?

- What security requirements will your office have?

Once you've assessed your space requirements, you can consider the options your home provides. Look carefully—there may be alternatives you hadn't seen before. Obviously, a gigantic spare (and conveniently empty) room would be ideal, provided it meets other requirements for your efficiency. If you are so fortunate as to have a separate space to transform into an office, consider yourself blessed. Otherwise, look for creative ways to work with what you've got.

Some telecommuters share space in a seldom used room, such as a guest room or even the dining room (unless you entertain frequently or don't have a table in the kitchen). Sharing a space in a room such as a family room or living room is usually less desirable, since these rooms usually are used by other people in your house and maintaining separation can be difficult. However, if you must have an arrangement like this, there are some great furniture solutions that provide an efficient "office in a box" that closes neatly when not in use and can easily be mistaken for an armoire. This type of solution also can work as a customized built-in arrangement in a closet, providing the dedicated office you need for working within the confines of limited space and with the advantage of having it "gone" when you close the door.

Using a section of your bedroom for your office is usually an undesirable option, since the mingling of work and sleep are not conducive to doing either one very well. If you absolutely must use a section of your bedroom or another room with a primary purpose other than housing your office, be sure to use a partition of some sort

(or an "office in a box") so you provide the necessary separation between your professional life and your personal life.

A final thought to consider: Wherever you decide to locate your
office, be sure it's in a place where you WANT to work. A large, cav-
ernous basement may appear to provide more space than you'll ever
need; however, if it's dark, windowless, damp, or gives you the
creeps, it certainly won't beckon to you and contribute to your motivation. The same is true for a cozy attic office—if you feel claustro-
phobic and always on the verge of a panic attack or heat stroke.
Everything else you do to create focus, organization, systems, and
support for your telecommuting success will be undermined by an
office that you hate. So, create an office in your home that balances
and combines requirements for appropriate space, suitable convenience, necessary separation, and personal comfort.

TIP²

✓ If you're just establishing your home office or need to reevaluate
  the location of your existing office, make a list of everything
  you need, such as furniture, equipment, supplies, files, resource
  materials, etc. (Tip 101).

✓ Create an office layout and determine your space requirements.

✓ Based on the space options in your home, consider the pros and
  cons of each option in light of the factors discussed above.

✓ If you're already ensconced in your home office, reassess how
  well it's working for you in terms of needed space, access, separation, security, etc. Consider a change or enhancements if your
  office is not all you thought it was cracked up to be.

TRANSFER IT PROMPTLY TO IMPROVE PERFORMANCE

13 Draw a Clear Line Between Your Work and Living Space

More than likely, you won't have an ideal location for your home office unless you: (1) are fortunate enough to have designed your home with this in mind; (2) have the luxury of renovating or remodeling to create an ideal work space; (3) have a former carriage house on your property that lends itself perfectly to your needs; or (4) you have a huge house and a large, empty room (with a bathroom, small kitchen, lots of windows, plenty of electrical outlets, multiple telephone jacks, etc.) that yearns to function as an office. If none of these scenarios describes your situation, you have lots of company—and need to improvise! Situating your office within your home with a clear demarcation between office and home is one of your biggest challenges and most critical requirements for successful telecommuting.

To whatever extent possible, your office should be removed from the activities and distractions of your home and family. If, however, you're using a spare bedroom or other location that's not in a separate wing of your mansion, consider a few steps to promote real and psychological separation:

- Install a solid (versus hollow) door to buffer distracting sounds.

- Add additional soundproofing with cork board on your walls (very functional, as well!).

- Use carpeting that's different from the rest of your house (and functional for use with office furniture and equipment: thick or shag carpeting was not designed for use with casters on office chairs).

- Keep your personal business matters (mail, checkbook, files, etc.) in a separate location so your office is clearly a work-related space only.

Be sure that your soundproofing blocks out distracting sounds (like your children, assuming someone else is managing their care) but still lets you hear sounds that are important to your work (like the doorbell when an express delivery arrives). One way to stay connected while removed from the epicenter of activity in your home is to use an intercom or room monitor. This alerts you to the doorbell or a true family emergency that would demand your attention whether you were telecommuting or in an office 10 miles away.

Because your office is ever-present in your home and so easily accessible, you may benefit from learning ways to psychologically separate your work life and your home life, as well. One way to draw a psychological line between work and home is to end your workday with a ritual that signals you to focus on the rest of your life. Hopefully, you have a door you can close; discipline yourself to leave it closed until the next workday. Other end-of-day ritual and techniques successful telecommuters use to transition to a nonwork mindset include:

- End the workday with a 15-minute planning session for the next day's work.
- Take a walk.
- Head out to the gym for a workout.
- Spend a few minutes of "how was your day" sharing time with your spouse or kids.
- Have a snack.
- Change clothes.
- Make a small dent in your *Reading in-box (or treat yourself to some light, nonwork reading).

TIP²

Identify:

3 Sources of distraction that come from your home, your personal life, or your family.

2 Things about your office that make it hard for you to concentrate or get started with work.

1 Major barrier to your ability to "close the office door" in your mind at the end of your work day.

Consider ways to overcome these obstacles and implement solutions for at least two of them today.

TRANSFER IT PROMPTLY TO IMPROVE PERFORMANCE

14 Determine the Best Address for Your Home Office

Just because your office is in your home doesn't mean your home address also should serve as your business address. True, your mail reaches you more directly if it's dropped in your home mailbox, and packages left on your doorstep easily are accessible. However, there are several disadvantages that you should consider.

If you live in an apartment, condominium complex, or gated community, mail might not be delivered directly to your door. Additionally, delivery services sometimes face delivery restrictions in these situations. A package delivered to the property management office on Friday afternoon might not be accessible to you until Monday if you can't retrieve it before the office closes. If packages can be delivered directly to your doorstep, they often will be left there for days if you're traveling or away on vacation—and the mail can begin spilling out of your mailbox in a short period of time while you're away. So, if you receive your mail at home, you'll probably need to ask someone to retrieve it or ask the post office to hold it when you're out of town. This can prove to be a big nuisance if you travel more than occasionally.

Some telecommuters prefer to keep their home address out of their business dealings for other reasons, as well. You might not want your home address to be public information. If you need to include your mailing/shipping address on your letterhead, business card, envelopes, e-mail or fax cover page, your home address inherently becomes public information. Should this be unacceptable for any reason, you may elect to use an entirely different address.

If you opt to use an address other than your home address, there are several options: (1) a post office box—although this is problematic for most express or package delivery needs since many shippers will not deliver to post office boxes; (2) post office box for mail and home address for packages (do you have room on your business card for two addresses?); (3) an executive suite location with ship-and-receive services; (4) a full-service ship-and-receive location (e.g., Mailboxes, Etc., The Package Store, etc.). The off-site ship-and-receive alternatives should offer staffed facilities that provide signatures, tracking and storage for your mail and packages, as well as after-hours access to your mail. Dedicated ship-and-receive services seem to provide the best combination of options and flexibility for a telecommuter with mounds of mail, occasional packages and express shipments, and varying degrees of travel.

TIP^2

Do you need a change of address? Review the types of mail and packages you receive, how you receive them and problems you encounter. If you need to change your address, check the yellow pages for options (Mailbox Rental and Receiving) or create a new version of your home address.

TRANSFER IT PROMPTLY TO IMPROVE PERFORMANCE

15 Design Your Office for Efficiency

If even the thought of designing your office makes you panic or begin fantasizing about hiring an interior designer to make it magically appear, this might be an area where you do need some expert assistance. Keep in mind, however, that you ultimately must think through your equipment and furniture needs, space limitations, necessary work flow and requirements, as well as your individual work style. It's unlikely you'll get what you need if you attempt to abdicate completely and trust anyone else to design an office that will work for you. So whether you're planning to work with a design expert or pull together the components of an efficient office on your own, you'll need to give careful consideration to a few key issues:

- What type of work do you do, how does your work flow, what does a typical day consist of in terms of work activities?

- What information, resources, references, files, etc. must you typically access throughout your work day?

- What equipment is critical to your successfully and efficiently accomplishing your work?

Answering these questions leads to a determination of the type of furniture and storage space you need, how much space it will require, and how it will best be placed in your office. If you've already created a floor plan (Tip 12), you know that assessing your needs and designing an office plan sometimes results in reconsidering your office location. Once you've settled on the location, however, you want to achieve the most efficient use of the available space.

With limited space, a modular furniture system might be best. If you have more space available, a U-shape or L-shape design often promotes wonderful efficiency and access to equipment and information. From where I currently sit, I can—without leaving my chair—use my computer; operate a four-line telephone; grab current project files; reach for paper clips, writing implements, the calculator, the stapler, tape, etc.; dictate a quick thought or letter; participate in a videoconference; retrieve output from both my laser printer and my fax machine; and shred any of that output in the paper shredder! While sitting for hours isn't such a great thing (Tip 24), efficiency in the design of your work space is fundamental to your success as a telecommuter. Without an office that promotes efficiency, you're likely to either fail or make yourself crazy—or both!

- 🗐 Make a list of all the things (e.g., equipment, files, information, supplies) you access in a typical day.
- 🗐 Design (or redesign) your work space to make all of those things easily available.
- 🗐 Look around for "dead" space—on the walls, under/on/above/behind your desk—that you can use more effectively to hang, stack, box, shelve, or file the things you need.

TRANSFER IT PROMPTLY TO IMPROVE PERFORMANCE

16 Design Your Office for Good Health

Any way you cut it, you'll spend a lot of time in your office. So it behooves you to make it not only a safe and pleasant place but also an environment that promotes good health. This is desirable since unhealthy situations and habits can lead to inconvenience, expense, and pain for you—and your employer is not likely to be thrilled with a workers' compensation claim that is avoidable. To begin, there are any number of steps you can take personally to ensure that you stay healthy (Tip 23) and that your office is safe (Tip 17). Let's focus here on how the design of your office can support your sustained good health and continued productivity. Keep these key things in mind when you select your office space, choose your equipment, and design your office layout:

- If you don't have plenty of natural, northern **light** streaming into your office, supplement with a good balance of ambient (bright, indirect light for the room) and task (direct light on your work space) lighting. Avoid bright sunlight, lighting directed at your computer monitor, or bright light directed at your eyes.

- Work at a **temperature** that keeps you alert and comfortable while ensuring a good supply of fresh air (just open the window!—or install a ceiling fan). Also, too little or too much humidity can be uncomfortable and should be avoided. Your list of essential office equipment may need to include a humidifier or dehumidifier.

- If your office design is highly efficient and you're sitting a lot, a proper fitting **chair** is essential (Tip 93). Aside from the **adjustability** you'll want in your chair, look for work surfaces that adjust to different heights and angles. If possible, consider a stand-up work surface, provided you can access the needed equipment and information to maintain efficiency.

- Carefully select a **computer** keyboard and mouse that is suited to your needs and minimizes the pitfalls that come with computer territory. And be sure your monitor is large enough and clear enough to avoid eye strain. While your notebook computer is great for traveling, it's not the best option for significant office use. If your notebook is your primary computer and you like having everything in one machine, consider a docking system or port replicator that enables you to use a more appropriate monitor and keyboard for extensive office computing.

- Assuming you spend any amount of time on the telephone, don't even debate with yourself—buy a **headset** that gets that telephone off of your shoulder and frees your hands for other productive work (Tip 92). The savings in neck strain and raging headaches will make your headset one of the most cost-effective investments in your entire office.

 TIP²

Select one aspect of your environment (air, light) and one aspect of your equipment that can be changed to improve the health level of your work space. Implement it now (open the window, adjust your chair height), or schedule execution of your improvement ideas as quickly as possible.

TRANSFER IT PROMPTLY TO IMPROVE PERFORMANCE

 Be Your Own OSHA Inspector

The local OSHA (Occupational Safety and Health Administration) inspector may not be on your list of external partners and is not likely to ever visit your home office. And though your employer may not conduct an on-site check of your office for conformance to safety, security, or design standards, office safety should not be an issue you overlook. Many of the basic safety guidelines applicable to corporate offices are relevant to your home office, too. While your employer may provide guidelines to guard against liability challenges and worker compensation claims, you should monitor compliance with office safety standards to protect your personal well-being and to guard against damage to your property. Compromising either objective potentially results in situations that preclude you from working.

Exercise diligence with regard to safety in your home office and monitor how your office stacks up against these basic guidelines:

❏ Aisles/walkways clear of boxes, chairs, wastebaskets, etc.

❏ Files not top-heavy (e.g., empty drawers on bottom, full drawers on top).

❏ Boxes of papers, files, books not stored on top of cabinets, files, window sills, equipment.

❏ First aid kit easily accessible.

❏ Equipment turned off when not in use.

❏ Restricted access to equipment (paper cutter, utility knife, etc.) potentially harmful to children.

❏ Pencils pointing down in pencil holders.

❏ Availability of ladder or appropriate step stool.

❏ Phone numbers for local emergency services posted on each phone.

❏ Electrical cords in good condition (not frayed).

❏ Electrical cords located away from heating sources and working/walking areas.

❏ Electrical equipment located away from water source.

❏ No use of unnecessary, inappropriate, or excessive numbers of extension cords.

❏ All electrical equipment and appliances grounded (use of three-pronged plugs).

❏ Use of appropriate power-surge protection equipment.

❏ Fire extinguisher easily accessible to office and in working order.

❏ Appropriate ventilation for good health and to vent fumes from equipment or materials.

❏ Flammable liquids stored properly.

❏ Adequate lighting for type of work performed.

For additional information or more detailed guidelines, contact your local Department of Labor or OSHA office, or access OSHA on-line at *www.osha.gov.*

TIP²

☑ Use the checklist above to evaluate the "safety correctness" of your office.

☑ Are there any areas of vulnerability? Pay particular attention to areas of potential significant hazard (fire risk, chemical exposure, etc.).

☑ Take immediate steps to correct any dangerous conditions in your office by relocating offending materials or by calling an appropriate service provider to correct the situation.

☑ On a related issue, review your homeowner's insurance or renter's policy to ensure you have adequate coverage for losses of structure or contents associated with your home office (Tip 99).

TRANSFER IT PROMPTLY TO IMPROVE PERFORMANCE

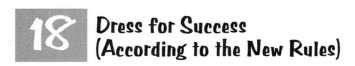

18 Dress for Success (According to the New Rules)

With the advent of casual dress, dressing for success certainly has evolved over the last decade. This could not be more true than for telecommuting, where dress for success rules are driven by what works best for you—what makes you feel best and what helps you work best. And until videoconferencing and videophones are more prevalent in the telecommuting workplace, when you're working at home, you're dressing for you and you alone. (Good news: Even if you utilize video communication, it only matters how you look from the waist up!)

The media continue to publish articles about telecommuting with fanciful pictures of telecommuters wearing bathrobes and bunny slippers or floating in a swimming pool with a drink and a notebook computer. Unfortunately, this perpetuates the myth that telecommuting is an informal, laid-back adventure in relaxation with only occasional interruptions of work. Do not be misled by these unrealistic images! Most telecommuters find the relaxation/interruption equation to be completely reversed. As for the bathrobe and slippers, if this wardrobe choice helps you feel focused, energized, and professional, by all means do it. More frequently, however, effective telecommuters choose comfortable attire (sweats, jeans, shorts, T-shirts, sensible shoes). Some telecommuters use dress to help establish a mindset for work, so for them donning a shirt and tie or a dress contributes to a productive workday. The same issues of individual style and psychological need influence other choices, such as shaving and wearing makeup. If it helps you work more productively, do it; otherwise, save the time for more critical activities. One telecommuter I know really feels there's a connection between how he looks and how he works ("If I feel sloppy, chances are I will do sloppy work"), so he won't start his work day until he's showered, shaved, and dressed (the equivalent of business casual). Remember, whatever works for you is the right solution for you.

If meetings with clients, suppliers, or colleagues may be part of your day, dressing appropriately for such meetings might determine your daily wardrobe. In any case, you should dress once and avoid outfit changes midday, since this is a waste of precious time.

 TIP²

Along the wardrobe continuum from bunny slippers to business suit, a range of options are available to you. Make your choices based on NEED (any meetings today?), STYLE (can you take yourself seriously in your bathrobe?), and COMFORT (what feels both relaxed and energizing and isn't a barrier to your work?). Consider your wardrobe options. Are your choices contributing to your overall productivity? If not, decide now on ways to improve your focus, effectiveness, and time efficiency when you get dressed and prepare for work each day.

TRANSFER IT PROMPTLY TO IMPROVE PERFORMANCE

Make a Habit of Avoiding Bad Habits

Poor work habits are a problem for anyone, since they erode productivity, compromise effectiveness, and—eventually—degrade motivation. All of these factors are exacerbated for the telecommuter because of the independence and isolation characteristic of remote work. The successful telecommuter makes it a habit to plan, organize, and execute work so that bad habits are avoided.

Do bad habits plague you? Consider whether any of these have crept into your work, day, or life:

* Sleeping longer and starting your work day later than you should.

* Not regularly reviewing your priorities and updating your action list.

* Longer work breaks or lunch breaks than are necessary (or breaks that evolve into social, shopping, or snoozing activities).

* Watching TV when you should be working.

* Consuming alcoholic beverages, drugs, or unhealthy food during the workday.

* Working constantly.

* Looking, feeling—and working—like a slob (generally, leave pajamas and bunny slippers in the bedroom—and don't let your personal hygiene completely lapse!).

* Excessive *or* insufficient amounts of planning, organizing, filing, Internet surfing, exercising, eating, relaxing, meditating, networking.

Of course, none of these habits is innately bad unless it becomes extreme enough to be a detriment to your effectiveness. Keep in mind (something else your mother may have mentioned!) that the "rule of moderation" applies here—even a strength in excess becomes a weakness. Much as you might believe Mae West's maxim "Too much of a good thing is wonderful!", it's not likely she was referring to work issues or habits. Also, remember that you shouldn't try to transform all of your bad habits to good habits at once. Once again, moderation is the rule.

TIP²

Make a list of the habits you want to change. Select one to change today:

- ☹ Think about what causes the bad habit or what keeps you from changing it.
- ☹ Analyze the process or precipitating incidents that activate the bad habit.
- ☺ Visualize the new habit and imagine how you'll feel and behave.
- ☺ Identify the steps that will provide a different response to what's activating the bad habit.
- ☺ Eliminate obstacles to the new habit (get the futon out of your office!).
- ☺ Provide interim rewards to yourself as you progress to full integration of the new habit.

Note on your calendar when you plan to implement this change process for other bad habits on your list. Don't overwhelm yourself, but be dogged in your determination and attack the most counterproductive ones first.

TRANSFER IT PROMPTLY TO IMPROVE PERFORMANCE

20 Reject the Refrigerator that Beckons You

One of the biggest struggles some telecommuters face is the refrigerator—it seems, at times, to call out your name, be needy of your attention, and be anxious to dispense its contents. However reasonable, analytical, or planful you may otherwise be, all semblance of these fine traits may dissipate when you walk within 20 feet of your refrigerator (or any other place where delectable edibles are stashed). Why is this? We're not all a bunch of undisciplined telecommuting food junkies. Rather, the reasons are varied—some overeat out of nervousness, the need for a break, procrastination, and—sometimes—as a response to hunger. However, the temptation is not just to overeat, but to eat badly. This is more often a result of poor planning (nothing healthy in the refrigerator) or laziness (a high-fat, prepackaged entree cooked for 3 minutes in the microwave is easier than just about anything healthy, or so it seems). And then there are the workaholic telecommuters who simply let the day fly by without eating much of anything. These folks aren't as fat, but nor are they any healthier.

Your refrigerator is like so many other things in life—you get out of it what you put into it. So, start your "refrigerator control" program by committing to a healthy lifestyle and diet. From there, decide on the types of healthy foods that (1) you enjoy and will eat; (2) are not excessively time-consuming to prepare; (3) will provide a nutritionally balanced, taste-pleasing variety of meal and snack options. Purchase the healthy foods you've chosen and eliminate, wherever possible, any sources of unhealthy foods in your kitchen (or your office, if you're one of those who stockpiles goodies like a squirrel preparing for winter!).

Knowing that tempting foods may be impossible to completely eradicate from your home (if you live with other people, occasionally receive yummy gifts, or maintain your supply of excess Halloween candy right through the Christmas cookie season until the onslaught of Easter candy), here are a few ways to remind yourself about the virtues of planful and controlled eating:

- As part of your weekly planning, decide on meal choices and snack options. Giving yourself choices, within a range of preestablished guidelines and limits, won't make you feel so regimented and restricted.

- Don't eat randomly—schedule your snack breaks or snack only when you're hungry.

- Don't hang around the kitchen while you eat (food seems to yearn for more food!). You probably need a change of scenery, anyway. Have lunch on your deck, munch on carrot sticks while you take a short walk, or drink a glass of juice while doing your on-line banking.

- If you're a recovering overweight person, post a picture of your larger self on the refrigerator. Remembering how hard you worked to achieve the new, slighter you will dissuade you from overindulging.

➤ Cover your refrigerator with clippings from magazines and catalogs of people whose bodies you, too, can have if you avoid overeating. (This also will encourage you at a subconscious level to stay in better shape through exercise.)

➤ Post friendly (and large-print) reminders on the refrigerator:

"Over the lips—straight to the hips!"

"If it tastes good, spit it out!"

Bear in mind that a number of former telecommuters decided to return to a traditional office because they attributed their weight gain to working at home. So, while all of this emphasis on healthy eating may be good for you, it may also be essential to your satisfaction and success as a telecommuter.

TIP²

Make a commitment to healthier eating and having more control over your snacking. Begin by adding:

4 Healthy meal options to your grocery list

3 Healthy snack choices to your approved snack list

2 Motivational quotes or photos to your refrigerator door

1 Unhealthy item currently in your refrigerator to the trash bin

TRANSFER IT PROMPTLY TO IMPROVE PERFORMANCE

21 Work During Your Peak Energy Times

In an ideal world, you would work only when there is a harmonic convergence of time, energy, inspiration, and need. But since you must sometimes deliver your services at the convenience or demand of others, the timing of your work might not always align with the peaks in your motivation and energy levels. Whenever possible, however, it's helpful (to you and your employer/colleagues/clients/ partners) to work during your phases of high energy and to minimize certain types of work during dips in your energy level. If your circumstances provide any degree of flexibility on the timing of your work, begin by knowing the patterns of your energy level.

To determine your energy patterns, think about how you currently work: when you feel highly energized, when you feel that you'd love to (or you do!) just nod off for a nap, when you find yourself tackling complex tasks, when you feel that talking on the phone is the most challenging task you can undertake, etc. If you're not certain when you're more inclined toward certain types of work, keep a log for a week or so to track what work you do when. From this log, develop a profile of your energy and work patterns, and look for ways to leverage your patterns to maximize your productivity. Consider, also, the limitations on your ability to work during times of peak energy.

Unless your job is completely flexible or you are an individual contributor with minimal external contact, it's likely you'll have some constraints on how you manage your work and your energy. If you negotiated a telecommuting agreement with your employer, you may have committed to availability during specific hours of business operation. Certainly if you're providing customer service or support by phone, there will be certain times you're expected to be available (and coherent!). Also, if you work with people or support operations across multiple time zones, you'll need to manage your work and your energy with this in mind.

On the other hand, if you have lots of flexibility, you may join those of us who are natural-born night owls and able to accomplish enviable amounts of work through the night. Telecommuting often offers a range of options and degrees of flexibility with regard to how and when you complete your work. And without the commute, it's much easier to accommodate those bursts of energy at unusual hours.

As you balance the demands of your job with the reality of your energy patterns, don't forget about ways you can enhance your energy. Staying fit and healthy (Tip 23) will contribute to your overall energy level, while taking appropriate breaks throughout the day (Tip 24) can make a real difference in extending energy peaks for top performance.

It's not likely that the events of your typical day are ever completely within your control, so your ideal work schedule and pattern may seem a bit like a pipe dream. But, knowing when it's best for you to do different types of work and using this knowledge as a guide will allow you to achieve the best output for the energy you invest each day.

TIP²

Determine the discretionary time available in your daily schedule and consider the best use of the time based on your energy patterns. Add at least three action items to your schedule for specific activities at certain times based on your anticipated energy levels and the requirements of your job.

TRANSFER IT PROMPTLY TO IMPROVE PERFORMANCE

22 Make "the Rounds" for Efficient "Erranding"

Being a telecommuter, you're likely to resist unnecessary time in your car or any other mode of commuting. A reality of telecommuting life, however, is that some "erranding" is unavoidable and may in fact increase, since you are likely to be remote from corporate services. With this reality accepted, it's wise to avoid procrastination or inefficiency in your erranding and focus on accomplishing what you must in a minimum of time and with a minimum of effort. The following guidelines will help you incorporate efficient erranding into your day.

⊕ Avoid the temptation to ease your sense of isolation by socializing while running errands. Instead, avoid any face-to-face encounters where you can by banking electronically, ordering office supplies on-line and having them delivered, using courier or express delivery services whenever possible, and using your phone and fax whenever those walking fingers can save you time.

⊕ When you must get in your car and run errands personally, plan your route carefully by arranging stops geographically. Consult a map if necessary and look for alternative routing that minimizes your time out of the office.

☺ Use your drive time as productively as possible. Use your cellular phone to make calls that require minimum concentration (and very minimal notetaking!). Keep a list of key phone numbers handy in any vehicle you might use for errands (since you might not always remember your day planner, and accessing a phone number from your computer is a tricky task while driving). If making calls isn't an option, keep a microcassette recorder handy to record ideas that occur to you during mindless driving or to dictate letters, memos, monthly reports, etc. (or in my case, to dictate another tip!). Keep a pad of paper and pen or pencil in all of your vehicles so you always have at least a low-tech way to capture a thought and make your drive time as productive as possible.

☺ Be familiar with alternatives and options for your most common erranding needs. Toward this end, know where the latest pick-up times are for the mailboxes within a 10-mile or 10-block radius of your home (your local post office does not necessarily provide the latest pick-up time). Also, know or keep a list of the express service drop boxes and pick-up times in your area. (Even better—have express items or packages picked up at your office whenever possible.) If you frequently need other business services such as printing, copying, word processing, etc., be familiar with the options in your area and their times of operation, and know the backup option you'll exercise if your first choice is unavailable (which will happen only when you're operating under an incredibly tight deadline for a major project!).

TIP²

Make a list of your typical stops when you run errands. Review the list for at least two stops you can eliminate or minimize by using other options. Consider how you can improve the order in which you make your rounds to save time. Call either your local or central post office to locate the closest mailboxes with the latest pick-up times.

TRANSFER IT PROMPTLY TO IMPROVE PERFORMANCE

23 Stay Fit and Healthy

Once again, the "Rule of Mom" is the operational guide to staying fit and healthy: get plenty of rest; eat a balanced diet; don't forget to exercise, drink plenty of water, and take a multiple vitamin everyday. Putting aside everything you might read on this topic (and foregoing all the fancy equipment or the expensive health club membership), it really comes down to the fundamentals from Mom. Of course, Mom didn't explain the specifics of making this work for telecommuters, so read on!

I love the sections on sleep you find in any number of books about health, self-management, successful entrepreneurship, etc. They include long explanations of the value of sleep, with cute little self-quizzes to help you determine if you're getting enough sleep. In the spirit of efficiency, try this instead:

Q: Are you tired?
A: No—great!
A: Yes—you probably need to get more sleep.

Of course, you know all the benefits of sleep to your body and brain. So, if you need to sleep more, then just do it—everyday, because Mom was right also about our inability to stockpile those sleep hours! As for naps, whoever invented the concept of siesta was brilliant, and probably in tune with rhythms of the human body. Some people can take a 15-minute catnap midday and reenergize for the second half of a long day. If you're wired this way, give thanks for the good fortune of your telecommuting blessings, use part of your lunch break for that quick nap, and avoid compromising any of your commitments to availability during scheduled work hours.

Entire libraries can be filled with books about diet and healthy meals, so I'll leave it to you to find the best culinary solutions for your health needs. Be aware, however, that telecommuting easily can result in either not eating (the workaholic reigns and won't stop to eat!) or overeating (Tip 20). Neither is a good idea, and you'll need to be conscious of the effect your work has on your food consumption.

As for water consumption, it's an easy enough thing to do, certainly. But, like other things, it requires discipline. So, be creative: Add it to your daily task list, including a specific amount of water to consume. Get a water cooler for your office that's either easily accessible to your desk or provides you a good reason to get out of your chair to stretch and walk across the office (not to mention the exercise you'll get walking to the bathroom so often!). Reward yourself—select an incentive (food, quick visit with your kids, short phone call to a friend, etc.) you can earn for hitting water intake targets.

Of course you should exercise daily, and only you can make the commitment to creatively fit exercise into your day. Whether it's an invigorating way to start your day, to provide a midday break, or to make a transition out of your work day, it you don't plan it, it won't happen. Additionally, you can integrate exercise into your day by doing isometric exercises at your desk or using quick breaks for stretching. And don't forget to breathe—take several deep breaths periodically throughout the day. This is good for your body, your mind, AND your work.

TIP²

RIGHT NOW! Stand up, take three deep breaths, stretch your arms, and drink a large glass of water. Feel better? ☺

TRANSFER IT PROMPTLY TO IMPROVE PERFORMANCE

24 Take Breaks to Relax, Re-Energize, or Recover

Working in a traditional office, as I recall, seems to involve a long series of interruptions between which you try to complete your work. As a telecommuter, you'll probably find there are few interruptions if you've taken steps to manage this (Tip 34). More likely, you'll need to create opportunities for breaks from your work, whereas in BT (before telecommuting) days, you had constant breaks in your work flow.

People without telecommuting experience simply do not comprehend how focused and task-oriented a telecommuter can become, and, therefore, how easily an entire morning can fly by without even the thought of a break. As delightful as this sounds from a productivity perspective, it's really not healthy or ultimately productive to sit for extended periods of time, compromise liquid intake, and avoid breaks for the brain! Taking breaks is essential to good health, clear thinking, and the achievement of the much-sought-after balanced life (remember why you wanted to telecommute!).

Who would imagine that you might need to schedule a break?! If that's the only way you can be sure to fit breaks into your day, then do what it takes to make it happen. You might set a timer or plan a break at the end of a scheduled conference call or ask your spouse to retrieve you from your office at a designated time. You also can use other activities to prompt a break—refill your water glass, take your designated 3-minute stretch break each hour, let the dog outside for a few minutes, throw a load of clothes in the washer, have a quick juice break with your spouse, or surprise your kids with a quick hug.

Because we typically work in high-productivity work cultures and because telecommuters are prone to workaholism, the notion of taking *and enjoying* breaks requires moving beyond the sense of guilt often wired into our thinking. And, of course, many of the activities you might choose for your breaks can transform (if extended unreasonably) into time wasters. So, balance and discipline are critical.

Remember that you take these breaks—whether they are quick, 3-minute breaks or several hours in length—for your sanity and for your survival as a productive telecommuter. With this in mind, learn to appreciate your breaks as an essential part of your balanced life and expand the following list of break activities to rejuvenate your mind and spirit:

➢ Take a walk (or take the dog for a walk).

➢ Call a friend.

➢ Send a electronic card to an e-mail buddy.

➢ Take a musical interlude (play the piano, listen to a favorite CD, etc.).

➢ Read a nonbusiness magazine.

➢ Take a catnap.

➢ Surf the Internet (nonbusiness related).

➢ Have a romantic interlude.

➢ Catch headline news on radio or TV.

➤ Write a quick note you've wanted to send.

➤ Meet a friend for coffee or lunch.

➤ Meditate.

➤ Have a healthy snack.

➤ Sit . . . do nothing . . . just be (and breathe).

➤ Spend a few minutes with your pet.

➤ Visit your garden to enjoy the view, water plants, or dig in the dirt.

Schedule two breaks today. Decide now how you will spend your break times. Make a list of five other break activities you plan to enjoy during the next week.

TRANSFER IT PROMPTLY TO IMPROVE PERFORMANCE

25 Multi-Task to Maximize Your Productivity

Telecommuting will not save you from workaholic tendencies that rob you of the balance you need to be both professionally and personally successful. Nor will it eliminate the time and focus you must invest to achieve high performance levels in a demanding or challenging job. It will, however, afford you the flexibility to manage the competing demands on your time if you're open to approaching these demands creatively and learning how to integrate the many facets of your life. This requires maintaining a focus on your work that is not singular but, rather, encompassing—allowing for the reality that your work is important/vital/critical/primo, but also that your life is not one-dimensional (or shouldn't be!). Your work and the rest of your life must integrate and work well together to achieve ultimate success.

The first step toward integration is a handy little tool you can learn from your computer. There's a reason you're not still using a computer that does only one function at a time—it's slow, inefficient, and terribly frustrating. Your life will be, too, unless you master some basic skills in multitasking—the fine art of doing more than one thing at a time. My computer is persistently trying to access my e-mail service while I'm inputting these words. I don't have time to just sit while waiting for a response that isn't a busy signal—and you probably don't have that kind of time to waste either. There are lots of opportunities throughout your day to get more efficiency out of precious time. You should constantly look for, anticipate, and leverage these opportunities:

→ Have simple tasks or quick-read materials easily accessible during telephone "wait" times when you're stuck on hold.

→ Combine quick personal errands with your business errands if they're in the same vicinity or can save time. (For example, picking up your groceries midday when you're in the same area to pick up your mail may be very sensible if an evening trip to the grocery store will involve much more time due to an additional commute, increased crowds, etc. Assuming your schedule allows for this degree of flexibility during the day, you're more than likely to devote the available time in the evening to a work-related activity.)

→ Use some of your work breaks to make brief personal calls that aren't purely social (e.g., schedule an appointment with your doctor, hair stylist, etc.) or to do quick household tasks (make the bed, reshelve the kids' toys, get the breakfast dishes in the dishwasher, etc.).

→ When a conference call is long, somewhat unproductive and not necessarily demanding of your complete intellectual capacities (unfortunately, these virtual meetings still exist!), combine it with other office tasks that are not very distracting and not too noisy (e.g., reorganize your desk drawers, set up a new desktop lateral file system, backup your computer files, put postage on outgoing mail)—or tackle a personal task like trimming your nails. One word of caution: Be sure that your multi-tasking is essentially silent (or use the Mute button on your phone), since obvious multi-tasking can be distracting or insulting to callers.

TIP²

- 📄 Make a list (or keep a log for a week) detailing the tasks or activities you perform that have potential multi-tasking opportunities.
- 📄 Make another list of the tedious, time-consuming, low brainpower tasks that need to get done. Pick three opportunities to combine with the "gotta do" list and watch your output and efficiency begin to improve.
- 📄 Challenge yourself everyday to find just one more way to multitask and integrate the demands of your life.

TRANSFER IT PROMPTLY TO IMPROVE PERFORMANCE

26 Avoid the (Real or Perceived) Isolation Trap

If you willingly chose to telecommute, you undoubtedly yearned for the solitude and focus telecommuting would afford you. If telecommuting is an option you didn't voluntarily elect, these elements—along with the inherent isolation of telecommuting—are the reality of your world. Either way, you must balance the advantages of solitude with the potentially damaging affects of isolation and avoid a major threat to your effectiveness, emotional well-being, physical health, mental health, and ultimate success.

Isolation is a major complaint of telecommuters, even those who love the solitude. While everyone operates on a continuum of affiliation needs, and some of us need more or less of the types of interaction provided by a traditional office, everyone needs some amount of it. You must determine the right balance to meet your needs and proactively implement isolation avoidance techniques.

Keeping actively in touch with co-workers (Tip 51) is an important first step in managing your sense of isolation. There are specific ways you can stay connected and involved with your team in spite of being remote from them. Besides your team, it's important to stay in touch with the broader world (Tip 54) to stayed informed and to maintain a sense of connection to people, events, trends, changes and information beyond your team and your company. Here are a few key ways to help maintain those connections and overcome isolation:

- Use all the technology available to you—telephone, fax, e-mail, paging, Internet, teleconferencing, videoconferencing, web conferencing, electronic bulletin boards or conference rooms—to maintain communication, keep informed, stay visible.

- Schedule face-to-face meetings (breakfast or lunch meetings, walking or exercising together, playing tennis or golf, etc.) with co-workers, colleagues, associates, and friends on a regular basis.

- Join industry, trade, technical, or professional associations in your community.

- Participate in groups that support telecommuters and other home-based workers.

- Take frequent work breaks (Tip 24) to avoid the sense of solo plodding that leads to feelings of overwork, frustration, and isolation.

- Read professional and trade publications to keep abreast of developments in your field; technological changes affecting your industry and your job; and relevant trends that affect your work, industry, company, community, country, and world.

- Enroll in classes, seminars, and other professional development opportunities to keep yourself connected and to avoid lapses in your skill development (Tip 30).

- Teach a class or lead a seminar to keep you current in your field and keep you in tip-top shape for making sharp presentations.

- Volunteer for a service association in your community—it's hard to feel isolated when you're helping others.

Regardless of your level of comfort with solitude, recognize the negative impact of isolation on your life and your work, and actively plan activities and techniques to avoid the worst.

TIP²

Review your schedule for the next two weeks to assess the level of "isolation buster" activities on your calendar. Be sure your schedule reflects at least:

5 Work breaks throughout each day.

4 Networking events (meetings, phone calls, etc., with people other than your team).

3 Exercise opportunities each day. (Can you share these with someone?)

2 Opportunities to meet face-to-face with either your boss or a co-worker.

1 Professional development activity.

0 Days that hold the promise of no face-to-face human interaction. (The FedEx and UPS drivers do NOT count!)

TRANSFER IT PROMPTLY TO IMPROVE PERFORMANCE

27 Track Expenses and Expenditures

After you've cured yourself of the tendency to keep everything and you're more inclined to effectively manage the administrivia (Tip 10), it's important to be clear about which documents you will need to retain. In addition, you'll want to establish a streamline tracking and retention method that is easy to use, easily accessible, and relatively automatic.

Some of the guidelines associated with record retention will be provided by your employer. Your telecommuting agreement may stipulate certain types of records you're required to maintain. Of course, there are some of the more typical types of expense tracking requirements: mileage, tolls, travel, entertainment, etc. Other expense items, such as telephone, equipment, supplies, services, etc., may be directly billed to your employer or will require that you apply for reimbursement. If you're shelling out the money and submitting receipts for reimbursement, be aware of how easily you can lose track of the money you spend on your employer's behalf. Unless you have reliable systems *that you use consistently*, it's likely you'll come up short on reimbursements (and not even know it!). So unless you feel you're overpaid or want to consider your employer a charity to which you make donations, take a few key steps to ensure that your business expenses are reimbursed:

$ Keep a business mileage log in your vehicles and faithfully record any miles you drive and tolls you incur for business.

$ Establish a file, box, folder, or envelope in which all business-related receipts can be dropped in each day (this, of course, assumes you *will* be certain to get a receipt for everything!).

$ Use either a computer- or paper-based system (whichever you'll actually use) for tracking expenses and preparing reimbursement requests.

$ If not required by your employer, set up a regular schedule for yourself for submitting expense reports to your company—no less frequently than once a month, more often if you incur significant expenses.

$ Devise a tracking system for business expenses and receipts to use when traveling. At a minimum, have a file or envelope where you accumulate everything until you're back in the office. I've always tried to discipline myself to summarize expenses or prepare expense reports during my return flight or as an A-1 priority when returning to my office.

You also may want to track expenses associated with the use of a portion of your home for your office. If you're deducting these non-reimbursed home office expenses on your tax return, be sure to consult with your tax adviser as to the appropriateness of this for your circumstances and the proper way to document these expenses. At a minimum, you'll want to avoid any unnecessary "flagging" of yourself as a candidate for an IRS audit, as well as any unnecessary (and time-consuming) scrambling for documentation during the tax season.

TIP²

List the types of reimbursable and/or tax-deductible expenses you incur. How are you currently tracking these expenses, retaining associated receipts, submitting reimbursement requests, documenting for tax purposes, etc.? Revise (or create) the systems you need to ensure that all your expenses are captured and your expenditures reimbursed.

TRANSFER IT PROMPTLY TO IMPROVE PERFORMANCE

28 Simplify and Improve Continuously

It's critical to the efficiency and effectiveness of telecommuters to remember the simplification and time-saving rule, "If it ain't broke, don't fix it!" Because there's usually no one else around to handle improvements to systems, processes, procedures, etc., you'll be stuck implementing any changes you envision. This can be a major time drain and focus detractor and should, therefore, be avoided . . . unless something *really* is in need of change. In this case, your effort should be directed toward solutions that truly simplify your work and your life. And while you shouldn't wile away your day redesigning the color coding of your files or reorganizing your library according to the Dewey Decimal system, you should be constantly looking for ways to streamline, simplify, clarify, uncomplicate, uncloud, and unencumber your work and the way you do it.

Periodically assess how your systems, processes, and work flow are working by asking yourself which tasks take more time, consume more energy, cause more frustration, or result in more cursing than you'd like. (One of my telecommuting colleagues uses his personal "annual retreat" as a time to review systems and processes in his office, as well as to re-evaluate strategic issues such as focus, business goals, etc.) Then analyze how you handle those tasks and how the related support systems, tools, and information are aligned. Also look for signs of simplification and improvement opportunities if you observe:

- Clutter on your desk or surrounding your work area.
- Unnecessary redundancies in your tracking or documentation systems.
- Huge backlogs of filing. (Do you really need to keep it all?)
- Any amount of time spent looking for things (in drawers, files, boxes, closets, briefcases, or on your desk) that you need to access routinely and should be able to put your hands on instantly.
- "Lost" files (e.g., you just can't find them) on your computer or on backup disks.
- Outdated software that causes incompatibility problems with the systems and documents used by other people with whom you work.
- The use of fancy files, labels, packaging, etc. that are nice but not essential.
- Extra errand running for "one-off" or forgotten items.
- Continual rework on specific functions or tasks.
- Tendencies on your part to complete tasks to a state of perfection.

TIP²

Identify—and act on:

3 Critical tasks that you know could be simplified—schedule on your calendar time to create and implement simplification steps to address these situations.

2 Areas in your office that should be redesigned to improve your efficiency—decide how and when you'll take care of these.

1 Pile or drawer of cluttered, backlogged, or unread items that you keep stumbling over—get rid of it now!

TRANSFER IT PROMPTLY TO IMPROVE PERFORMANCE

29 Reward Yourself and Celebrate Successes

It's easy to forget about the value of rewards. And if you do remember to acknowledge, thank, and reward those who help you, it's easy to forget YOURSELF in the process. But inherent in the solo work of a telecommuter is the need to be cognizant of self-management issues to include rewards— for completing a major project, attaining a goal, hitting a significant milestone, surviving a really stressful week, re-taining a critical customer, landing a major new account, etc. It's es-sential that you find appropriate and meaningful ways to celebrate your successes and provide incentives and rewards because:

1. You're human and need these things.

2. Others may not be aware of your accomplishments—at least "in the moment"—and won't be in a position to provide a virtual pat on the back.

3. Your continued motivation, determination, perseverance and psychic energy will be greatly enhanced.

Without distracting yourself with a long, protracted process to devise a reward scheme for yourself, begin by making a brief list of rewards that are appropriate for different types of achievements and are meaningful to you. Combined with that, devise ways to celebrate your successes—a little bit of celebration along the way makes the daily grind tolerable and will help you feel as if it's all worth while. Your list of rewards and celebration rituals will be uniquely yours. But to help you get started, here are a few ways other telecommuters gives themselves kudos:

! A nice dinner at a new or favorite restaurant

! Tickets to a concert or the theater

! A new book (and the time to read it)

! An afternoon off for a round of golf, time at the beach or a museum, a tennis match or pampering at the spa

! A new outfit (or sofa, case of wine, piece of art, etc.)

! A long weekend at a resort, in a remote fishing camp, skiing, sailing, hiking, camping with the kids

TIP²

Create your own list of wonderful rewards for good work and ways to celebrate your successes. Decide now how you'll earn at least three rewards (be specific about the achievements to justify the rewards) and pinpoint the next success milestone that will earn you a specific celebration activity. Post your performance targets and the corresponding rewards/celebrations in a visible place in your office. Keep your longer list of rewards and celebrations wherever you document and track your goals. Learn to use rewards and incentives in the way that best motivates and sustains you.

TRANSFER IT PROMPTLY TO IMPROVE PERFORMANCE

30 Take Responsibility for Developing New Skills and Managing Your Career

As a telecommuter, your skill development and career management may suffer if you do not champion your own cause. While the amount of money corporations spend on training and investing in their human capital generally is increasing, this seems to be concurrent with an increased emphasis on self-responsibility for skill development. Further, with the rate at which people are changing jobs, careers, and employers and are being caught in merger/acquisition situations, it's no longer wise to trust your professional development plans and career management to your "employer du jour." Finally, the unique skills you require to successfully telecommute (Tip 1) may necessitate specific skill development efforts you might need to locate and/or fund at your own initiative. As for the management of your career, no one has as great a vested interest as you, so don't entrust this important task to anyone else.

So, beyond being a champion to access corporate resources, you may very well need to identify development needs, locate resources, and purchase what you need on your own. This is very consistent with the growing trend toward self-responsibility for learning and career management. *Fast Company* magazine refers to this as "The Brand Called You"™. This thinking is based on the philosophy and attitude that you're always self-employed and, for a time, you may find yourself on some company's payroll. Regardless of how your income reaches you, you remain ultimately responsible for addressing your skill and career development needs—both for your telecommuting function and for the job-specific aspects of your position.

So what are your needs?

✔ Begin first by looking at the job you're currently doing—what skills and competencies are essential for success?

✔ How do you stack up against those requirements?

✔ What problems are you experiencing, or what skill deficiencies have you identified for the telecommuting role you're in currently?

✔ What additional skills must you develop to achieve the level of success you desire?

✔ Beyond your current job, what do you expect to be doing (or want to do) for the next five years?

✔ What skill deficits or barriers currently compromise your ability to move in that direction or be successful?

Whether it's a move to management, sales, a line position, an individual contributor role or is a complete job change, an industry switch, or a move to self-employment, you're likely to have some deficiencies that are obstacles. Or you could be planning a fairly stable job picture for the foreseeable future and simply want to ensure that you remain competitive, marketable, knowledgeable, or challenged by your work. Either way, identifying your needs will help you craft a development plan and strategy for YOU, INC. Without a plan that you manage, you entrust your future and your prosperity to someone else. This is always a risky course of action.

TIP²

Make a list of your weaknesses relative to the skills needed for your current job and your ability to function well as a telecommuter.

What developmental resources can close any gaps you've identified? To identify appropriate resources for eliminating any skill deficits, talk to your boss or someone in human resources, contact the executive development division of a local university, or search the Internet for training options you can access through your company or on your own.

TRANSFER IT PROMPTLY TO IMPROVE PERFORMANCE

Working Well with Your Family

31 Negotiate Expectations and Agreements

The first thing you and your family should be in rock-solid agreement on is your decision to telecommute. This may be a major change to the lifestyle and day-to-day routine in your household, so don't underestimate the impact telecommuting will have on everyone involved. If your decision is more of a directive than a choice, you'll need to be even more careful in formulating agreements and dealing with issues, feelings, fears, concerns—those of your family *and* your own.

Without clear agreements established at the outset, you're likely to stumble through misunderstandings, hurt feelings, productivity drains, declines in marital bliss, and unnecessary stress. While you may have more structured, as well as spontaneous, opportunities to participate with your family, your presence in a home office can send confusing signals regarding your availability or accessibility. Many of the joys and advantages of telecommuting quickly dissipate when the expectations of your family are not aligned with either your expectations or your work requirements. Being diligent about addressing potential conflict proactively and reaching agreements productively will serve you well in your quest to be a successful telecommuter.

Being clear about where and when you'll work are fundamental issues to be agreed upon initially. If your office occupies a space separate from the rest of your home, this simplifies things. If, however, your office will occupy some space that is or previously was shared by other family members, your "squatter rights" won't necessarily eliminate conflict regarding use of the space. Access others will have to your office, when that can occur, and how the space (and anything in it) can be used by your family will need to be discussed in detail.

When you will require dedicated work time is another important issue that necessitates a clear agreement. You may have fairly firm work hours or require some flexibility for meetings, conference calls, international calls, etc., during nontraditional work hours. As much as possible, anticipate your requirements so you can have agreements in place—along with agreements to renegotiate as your needs and circumstances change. For example, should you begin a project that involves international associates, you may require extensive phone time with another part of the globe at some unusual (or inconvenient) times for your family. Anticipate this, whenever possible, and negotiate agreements in advance.

As with negotiation and goal-setting discussions you may have with your manager and colleagues, don't hesitate proactively to have corresponding discussions with your spouse, significant other, children, or household employees. Everyone will benefit from the clarity and frank discussion of needs and limitations, guidelines and options, dos and don'ts. Do yourself and those who share your life and space a big favor. Be clear about some basic things as a starting point:

- Work hours (established times or required flexibility)

- Interruptions (when, how, for what types of things)

- Work space (if it's share space, agree on where it starts/stops, how it's used, how it's maintained and organized)

- Household tasks (who does what and when)

- Childcare (who is responsible for what and when)

Consider where clear agreements are lacking with regard to your telecommuting arrangement. (Warning signs include sources of stress, conflict, loud disagreements, or unspoken fear of impending disaster!) Using the checklist above, schedule a time to negotiate an issue that requires a clear agreement. Follow the same process for other areas where clear agreements will contribute to your telecommuting success. Remember—sometimes it's those who care about you who will be the reminder (not so subtle, but vital!) of your commitment to balance and good health. You need to balance this concern with the realities of your work to ensure that both are recognized and reconciled.

 TIP²

To secure clear agreements with your family, be sure to:

✔ Explain clearly what you need or expect and why it's important to you or your work.

✔ Ask about issues, concerns, fears, feelings.

✔ Listen to and discuss your family's input.

✔ Mutually agree to a workable solution.

✔ Take notes on agreements and give everyone involved a copy.

✔ Schedule a follow-up time to confirm its working or revise the agreement if necessary.

TRANSFER IT PROMPTLY TO IMPROVE PERFORMANCE

32 Get Your Family on Your Team

Your family can work with you or against you when you telecommute, and it's better by far to have them working with you. As you identify the members of the broader support team that contributes to your success, your family is likely to be high on the list. Therefore, it's wise to acknowledge this, understand the dynamics of family support, and proactively enlist their support.

When you telecommute, your work world is inherently more apparent to your family than with more traditional work arrangements. Be conscious that your office occupies space in your home *and* the environment that others call home. Even if you have a clearly delineated work area that's removed from common areas in the house and you are very disciplined about maintaining separation from family during the work day, your proximity and presence cannot be forgotten completely. And the reality is that if you want to realize some of the personal benefits of telecommuting, you will be more visible at times (you might take a break to say hello to your kids when they get home from school; share your lunch break with your spouse; or, if you're a new parent, take a break to feed a newborn).

The increased visibility and additional opportunities for involvement with your family has a down side—family members might like being with you and may make demands for involvement that are detrimental to your work. This is when setting expectations and negotiating agreements (Tip 31) is helpful. As part of establishing (or renewing) your telecommuting arrangements, you must consider and incorporate your family in your planning. More important, involving them in your planning ensures that they understand your commitments to your work, your employer, yourself, and them. This is a key step in securing your family's commitment to be supportive members of your team.

Beyond the framework of your family's stated commitment to be supportive, look for ways to actively engage family members as bonafide teammates. A few techniques you might use:

- Find aspects of your work in which you can involve your family by getting their help (e.g., collating papers, stuffing envelopes, operating the copier, filing, unpacking supplies, organizing reference material, running errands, or just sharing problems and challenges and asking for ideas and input).

- Empower your family to help you monitor your track record relative to key professional and personal performance measures (e.g., sales results, call targets, exercise goals, life balance goals, time limits on hours in your office).

- Share the rewards and include your family in celebrations of your success (an end-of-day "office party" when major milestones are reached, a special shared meal to celebrate achievement of your quota for the month/quarter/year, a "brag board" where you post letters from customers or acknowledgments from your employer, or a special trip or vacation for the family when that big bonus check arrives).

TIP²

Identify and share with your family or significant other the following about your work-at-home arrangement:

3 Things that are positive for the relationship between you and them.

2 Things that you need their help with.

1 Way they can help you celebrate a recent success.

TRANSFER IT PROMPTLY TO IMPROVE PERFORMANCE

33 Manage and Minimize Distractions

Some distractions are self-initiated; they're caused by lack of focus (Tip 4), low motivation (Tip 7), or bad work habits (Tip 19). As with some forest fires, prevention is the key—and only you can prevent these types of distractions from wrecking your day, destroying your productivity, and undermining your telecommuting success. The same results can occur if you don't manage or minimize distractions caused by others (family, friends, visitors, pets, etc.).

Your family, in particular, has a unique ability to distract you from your work due to your presence and proximity. Negotiating agreements in advance (Tip 31) is a wise step, but managing distractions seems to be a challenge requiring on-going attention. Aside from the self-discipline you must have to avoid involvement in family or household matters during work hours, there are other strategies you can use to manage distractions:

- Establish specific rituals to begin your workday that clearly put you in a focused-on-work frame of mind.

- Evaluate interruptions from the perspectives of *seriousness* and *urgency*—stop working only if the issue rates high on both scales or the matter of urgency demands immediate attention on your part.

- Ignore the household chores (close doors, hide the laundry basket, remind yourself that no one will be visiting today—does it really matter if the bed isn't made or the sink is full of dishes?) until you've either completed your established work hours or accomplished all of your goals for the day.

- Don't answer the home phone (or screen calls using caller ID) and ignore the door bell (unless you're expecting an express shipment that requires your signature).

- Establish a sign or signal to your family when interruptions must be avoided (Tip 34).

- Use some of your scheduled work breaks to touch base with your family, check messages on the home phone, let the dog out, etc. so these do not become in-the-moment distractions.

- Turn the TV off, the stereo down, and ensure that sounds of shrieking/screaming/crying children (or spouse) cannot be monitored in your office.

TIP²

Decide today to minimize or eliminate three sources of distraction for you:

2 *Distractions that you directly control due to lack of focus or motivation.* Formulate a plan to manage the distraction you cause by identifying the source, diagnosing the cause, clarifying a measurement and reward system, and committing to a change NOW.

1 *Distraction that is caused by others.* Schedule time to talk with whoever else is responsible for distractions from your work and negotiate agreements (Tip 31) that will resolve the problem.

TRANSFER IT PROMPTLY TO IMPROVE PERFORMANCE

34 Establish Clear Interruption Rules

The proximity you have to your family while telecommuting greatly enhances opportunities for communication. This has clear advantages in terms of increased sharing of information, experiences, and time. However, the temptation for your family to capitalize on your accessibility can disrupt your concentration, compromise your productivity, and erode your patience. Because your presence is so apparent, the tendency to interrupt is understandable. For the same reason, it's important to specifically address the issue of interruptions with your family.

Basic guidelines regarding what constitutes a justifiable interruption is a good beginning. Even people who work in traditional offices often establish such guidelines, especially for their children ("Call me only if the problem involves fire, loss of blood, or you've already called 911 for any other reason!"). Otherwise, as you may have experienced, an incessant series of phone calls can result in an incessant litany proclaiming boredom, obnoxious siblings, or other problems completely unresolveable from a distance. However, your lack of distance should not be a reason to become involved in domestic situations that are better handled in other ways. It's often useful to provide similar guidelines for spouses who can become inordinately needy of your involvement in matters you wouldn't even know about if you weren't there.

Once you've established groundrules for a justifiable interruption, *how* the interruption is made is another point upon which to reach agreement. A sudden, loud—or tearful and whimpering—demand for your immediate attention may create an embarrassment to you and great frustration to the needy interrupter if you're in the midst of a conference call or negotiating a contract with an important prospect. So, set a clear method whereby whoever desperately needs you can communicate it. If you have a door to your office, remind everyone that it's there to be knocked on (quietly!). If you don't have a door, use some other visible method to convey that you're working (buy or make a "OPEN/CLOSED" sign to indicate when your virtual door is slightly ajar or closed tight).

To promote the notion of a gentle intrusion and the need for a possible delay in my response, I placed a little bell (like you might find on a counter in a small country store) on a shelf outside of my office. Even small children and a variety of service providers use my little bell quite consistently—and it's cheaper than installing a doorbell, less annoying than keeping the monitor on constantly, and provides a reasonable balance between immediate interruptions and a long-delayed response.

TIP²

Review how interruptions to your workday currently are made and/or how you would like them to be made. Establish two guidelines for *when* you can be interrupted and create a reasonable, family-friendly (or child-appropriate) method for *how* your attention can be captured when necessary. Set aside time on your schedule to discuss and reach agreement with your family.

TRANSFER IT PROMPTLY TO IMPROVE PERFORMANCE

35 Take Care of Childcare

There are few unalterable truths about much of anything, but about telecommuting there is one undeniable, nondebatable, nearly universal truth: Telecommuting is not a substitute for childcare. While you may have more time with your family (assuming you manage your workaholic tendencies and discipline yourself to stay out of your office when you should be with your family), the additional family time you have is derived primarily from your former commuting time.

Unfortunately, this is a great myth of telecommuting that still prevails (primarily among uninformed nontelecommuters). So, don't be surprised if people comment about your having more time with your family or being able to raise your children while working (a perception particularly held about women who telecommute). Anyone who has children knows that in most cases and when done properly, child-rearing requires a full-time commitment. And unless you have a part-time job, have a very flexible work schedule, and/or you require practically no sleep, combining two full-time jobs will produce dismal results for both.

Most corporate telecommuting agreements address the issue of childcare and will secure the telecommuter's commitment to provide adequate childcare arrangements. The options are the same as those for nontelecommuters: daycare, in-home nanny service, multiple baby-sitters, a grandparent or other relative, combination of school and childcare, etc. Some telecommuters find it easier (but certainly costlier) to have in-home nannies, since this avoids a commute to a childcare facility. Other telecommuters find that the distractions of children at home are too problematic and opt for out-of-home childcare. This option also provides for clear transitions into and out of your workday.

The best option for you is a function of

- Your budget—what can you afford?
- Your choices—is there a grandparent or other relative you can rely on and trust?
- Your psychological needs—do you need a work environment

that is free of any distracting sounds from your kids, or does it comfort you to know they're close by?

- Your work environment—is your office removed enough from activity centers in your home so that it's feasible to have family and work under one roof?

- Your job—can you run the risk of a screaming child being over-heard while you're on a conference call or negotiating a contract with a client?

- Your employer—is there a clear mandate that you provide full-time childcare during work hours?

One situation in which childcare and work may intersect is at times when your co-workers in a traditional office might otherwise need to take the day off. Even with full-time childcare and the best-laid backup plans, you're bound to face situations where a sick child or baby-sitter requires that you be at home with your children. In these cases, it's much easier for you to creatively integrate the demands of work and home on a short-term basis and keep your work flowing to some extent. As for the long-term, however, every telecommuter with children requiring full-time care needs a full-time and perma-nent childcare solution.

TIP²

- If you have young children who require the attention of a care provider, assess how well your current or projected childcare situation meets your needs. What current or potential problems are created by your childcare arrangements?

- How does your childcare solution support achievement of your job targets? How does it detract from your ability to be success-ful at work?

- Imagine some "worst case scenarios" and determine if you have adequate back-up arrangements in place to meet the demands of your job and your needs for childcare.

- What changes must you make to address the concerns you've identified?

36 If You Mix Childcare and Work (God Help You!)

One of the great myths of telecommuting is that it eliminates the need for childcare. True, you are likely to share more waking hours with your family if you telecommute. And you may be fortunate enough to have the flexibility (and necessary self-management) to adjust your work hours to participate in more of your children's activities and special events. But it's important to remember (and sometimes remind others) that caring well for children—especially young ones—is a demanding undertaking. Assuming someone is paying you to do a full-time job via telecommuting, it's not likely you'll handle either your job or parenting very well if you try to do both at the same time. Further, it is the clear (and reasonable) expectation of most employers of telecommuters that childcare arrangements are in place.

Some home-based business entrepreneurs are more inclined to combine childcare with a business enterprise. Although this, too, can be fraught with problems, the circumstances (independence, type of business, client expectations, financial pressures, etc.) may justify some integration of work and childcare. Still, it's certainly not easy, and it extracts a high price in terms of focus, energy, and productivity. The bottom line: Combining work and childcare is a risky, exasperating and potentially counterproductive venture. And if your employer has a specific policy (or implicit assumption) against it, it's a downright foolish venture.

If, in spite of all of the warnings, you undertake to juggle your job *and* your kids (and your employer supports this), it behooves you to learn ways to minimize the difficulties of doing so. Also, on days that you have a sick child or you're both stranded at home due to a weather (or traffic) obstacle, it's likely you'd miss the entire day of work if you commuted to a traditional office. One advantage you have as a telecommuter is that you can (depending on the age of your child, severity of the illness, etc.) continue to be productive on such days by keeping a few guidelines in mind:

- Avoid making or taking critical phone calls while children are in your office (unless they're old enough to honor commitments to keep quiet).

- If you must be on the phone, be sure you either disclose the situation to your caller or you are highly skilled in the lightning-speed use of the MUTE button on your phone.

- If your child still takes naps, utilize this quiet time to the greatest extent possible for phone time or focused work time.

- Designate a dedicated space and, if possible, a spare computer (Tip 37) in the office for kids to use.

- Have toys, games, whiteboard and markers, paper, crayons, and other creative play activities readily available. Involve your kids in some age-appropriate activity that enables them to help you or feel that they're helping, and remember that even toddlers love to sort and organize. One of my telecommuting friends keeps a VCR in his office (since he's a trainer), along with his trusty assortment of Disney videos for times when his children are in his office.

TIP²

If you have children or have occasion for children to visit your office, check your inventory of resources and activities you can make available quickly to keep little people entertained/distracted in your office. If your current options are limited, put together a KID box now; you're likely to really thank yourself at some point in the future.

TRANSFER IT PROMPTLY TO IMPROVE PERFORMANCE

37 "Take Your Children to Work" Guidelines

When you're working, you should do so without the distraction of children. However, telecommuting affords you the flexibility to integrate your family and your work on rare occasions. At the same time, it's important that you manage your balance between work and family so that you devote a reasonable amount of time to each of these important priorities in your life. When there does need to be some overlap, there are some creative techniques for incorporating children into your office so that it's a happy experience for all concerned. Additionally, familiarizing your children with your office and your work can minimize any resentment they may feel toward your work and enhance their understanding of and respect for what you do when you're ensconced in your office for hours at a time.

Having children in your office with you is likely to occur outside of your regular work hours (when you're desperately trying to get some critical work done or catch up on office chores during evening or weekend time). While this can be a fun time for your children and a life-saver for you, be careful to ensure that you're not trying to achieve the impossible, that your children are safe, and that everyone avoids any unnecessary frustration. Here are some ways to do this:

- Set some office rules and expectations for in-office behavior— consistent with the age of your children—regarding things like interruptions, noise levels, access to supplies, use of phones, etc.

- Designate a work space for your child, including a desk area, computer, calculator, writing tools, and other age-appropriate office items. (My 4-year old consumed huge amounts of time playing with an old 3-ring calendar binder containing all my unused pages and tabs, along with unused checks from canceled accounts, sticky notes, and brochures gathered at tradeshows, etc.).

- Be realistic about the need to childproof your office—make important documents inaccessible, lock or password-protect any computer equipment with critical files or software, put locks on drawers and cabinets, secure electrical cords to avoid tripping or shock hazards, get dangerous equipment out of reach (paper cutter, letter opener, knives, staplers, shredder, scissors).

- Secure bookcases, shelves, cabinets, lamps, etc. by bolting them to the floor if your children are still in the climbing phase.

- Remove small items and plants from view if your child is still in the chewing/choking phase.

- Involve your children as much as possible in your work—talk about what you do and why you enjoy it, show them what you do, take them with you when you can (on errands or deliveries or meetings, if appropriate) and let them help you in any way that's age-appropriate and fun.

TIP²

Look around your office and think with the mindset of a child (the age of your child/children).

- *Where are the places that hold potential for harm (but might look like fun)?* Take steps immediately to eliminate these before letting your child spend time in your office again.

- *Consider whether there's a way to designate or improve a dedicated work area for children.* It doesn't take much space or need to be fancy. (I created a nameplate for my daughter to place on her "desk" in my office, and it made her feel VERY important and involved!)

TRANSFER IT PROMPTLY TO IMPROVE PERFORMANCE

 ## The Shift to Home-Based Work with Older Children

Children who are born to telecommuters tend to grow up understanding and accepting the inherent rules of telecommuting for families. Except during phases of great attachment or separation anxiety (remember, they'd scream just as loudly if you were leaving to drive to an office), these children seem to take for granted that they have a parent working at home who cannot be disturbed during working hours. And note, these children also seem to have an internal clock that tells them when you should be done working!

The dynamics are different, however, if you begin telecommuting when your children are beyond the baby stage and have different expectations of parental presence and proximity. These children have learned from earlier experiences that having a parent around means that "kid time" is in full force. Beyond that, most young children like their parents and want to be with them. So, setting expectations and ground rules with these children is important to your telecommuting success and the happiness of both you and your children.

Begin by talking with your child about your home-based office, what you'll be doing there, and why you'll be working at home. Letting your children help you with some simple organizing tasks (such as sorting files folders by color) helps them become familiar with your office and comfortable with where you'll be. If you have been a full-time parent and are introducing a new child care arrangement to your child in conjunction with your new full-time job and your telecommuting situation, take great care to explain the reasons for this change, the benefits to both you and your child. More important, encourage questions, be open to discussing your child's questions and concerns as they emerge at unexpected times, and listen for opportunities to re-explain and reinforce your messages of support and love. As a parent, however, you've undoubtedly discovered by now that since children are constantly changing and evolving, so are the issues you need to deal with. So, consider it an ongoing discussion and take cues from your children about what to discuss and when they need to talk.

School-age children are better able to understand the role of work in your life and the need for separation, limitations and agreements. It's easier to negotiate agreements in these cases (Tip 31) and employ consequences and rewards where appropriate. Involvement of older children tends to be easier, so don't overlook ways to get your children on your team (Tip 32) and feeling that they have a role in your success.

Regardless of the ages of your older children and the level of involvement and cooperation you can reasonably expect from them, they certainly will resent you, your work, and your telecommuting arrangement if your work/life balance becomes unbalanced in favor of work. (And kids have an amazing detector for this malady!) You can't tell them too often that *they* are what's most important to you— your top priority and a major driver for your desire to telecommute. They'll tolerate (perhaps grudgingly at times—but, hey, they're kids!) a fair amount of the downside of your demanding, distracting job as long as they understand and benefit from the upside. Let them know often that you occasionally have time conflicts but that you never have priority conflicts.

- Make a list of five things you can do to let your children know that they are your #1 priority. Plan to do at least one of them today and add the others to your schedule for the near future.
- Ask your child to tell you two reasons why it's good that you work from home.

TRANSFER IT PROMPTLY TO IMPROVE PERFORMANCE

 ## Meeting the Challenge of Eldercare or Family Care

When unique or urgent family situations confront you, it's important to remember that while your job may provide extraordinary flexibility, it's still a job and you still have important work to do. The pressures of a demanding family situation may make it difficult to maintain the appropriate separation and focus you need. Additionally, you may face pressure and expectations from other family members who work in more traditional environments and who may have misperceptions about the degree of flexibility your work affords you. And while you may have done an admirable job of setting boundaries and ensuring that your work is respected (Tip 45), extenuating family circumstances can cause people to lose all semblance of rational thinking.

If you have a bona fide family care situation that requires additional attention from you for a period of time, you may need to take a leave of absence from work. In this case, you may be eligible for time off from work and should talk to your employer about this. While it may be tempting to continue working since your office is at home, don't short-change yourself, your family, or your work. Be realistic about the time and energy you'll need to devote to your family situation and plan accordingly.

If you're involved with an extended care situation, such as a disabled child or spouse or an ailing parent that resides with you, the factors that impact you and your handling of this situation are similar to those of childcare (Tip 35). You also must clearly assess the level of care the dependent family member requires and determine how much of that you can provide while continuing to meet the demands of your job. As with childcare, you may find it necessary to secure the services of a care provider. This may involve part-time or full-time in-home nursing services, as-needed companion care, elder daycare, or nursing home care.

Whatever your situation is or may become, keep in mind that telecommuting (in spite of its inherent flexibility) is *not* a substitute for family care or elder care services you may truly need. And while this might be clear to you, you'll also need to bear in mind that being forthright and assertive with family members may be necessary to ensure that the realities of telecommuting and the demands of your work are clearly understood. It's unwise (and ultimately unhealthy, unproductive, and potentially unprofitable) for you to let yourself and your work be taken advantage of when a family situation demands increased attention. Having this clear in your mind before a crisis occurs is useful, since clear thinking may not abound in the midst of a family crisis.

TIP²

Clearly articulate in your own mind what is and is not feasible with regard to family care and your availability of time and energy to help. Think about how you would present your position and parameters in such a case. If you're blessed enough to be free of such pressures now, jot down your thoughts to keep in a safe place and refer to it should you ever need the guidance of a rational mind.

TRANSFER IT PROMPTLY TO IMPROVE PERFORMANCE

40 Minimize Household and Family Stress

While telecommuting eliminates some of the stress associated with commuting to and working in a traditional workplace, it is certainly not a stress-free mode of working. Some of the advantages of increased proximity to your family and your office are offset by disadvantages that can be stressful to you and members of your household. Certainly you'll be more attuned to the problems and issues of your home and family, which can be an added source of stress you take with you to your office. At the same time, your family may be much more aware of and feel the tension and stress associated with some of your on-the-job issues and challenges:

- Deadline pressures
- Relationship problems with co-workers
- Unrelenting demands (from a nonstop phone, an overflowing in-box, an overloaded e-mail box)
- Falling short of goals
- Isolation and detachment from co-workers
- Being disorganized and feeling constantly "behind the power curve"

You and your family also will experience elevated levels of stress if there are unresolved problems within the home that are created by your telecommuting arrangement. Rather than wait for an issue to fester into a crisis (or to undermine your success with telecommuting), much of the typical stress telecommuters experience within their home and family can be averted by proactively setting expectations (Tip 31) on issues such as:

- Work time and space
- Interruptions
- Noise
- Orderliness and cleanliness
- Telephone protocols
- Visitors (during business hours)

Many telecommuters (and their families) also experience stress because of misunderstandings with regard to household responsibilities. Your presence and proximity do not constitute an inherent promise to take on additional household tasks, although it might be a natural assumption some people will make. Therefore, take great care to discuss and agree in advance who will handle responsibilities such as:

- Child care and family care
- Lawn maintenance/gardening
- Cleaning
- Laundry
- Lunch preparation/cleanup
- Answering the phones/door
- Cooking
- Shopping
- Errands
- Household financial management

 TIP^2

Since a great antidote for telecommuting stress is proactive and open dialogue, block off time on your calendar today to discuss and implement action steps to eliminate:

- A source of stress you create for your family (be sure to listen carefully).
- An area of stress you experience that your family can alleviate (be sure to be specific and clear).

Using effective issues resolution skills (Tip 42) is key to keep the focus on the problem while avoiding defensiveness and anger.

41 Working With and Around Your "4-Legged Children"

With or without children, if you have a pet in the house, you have some unique parent-like considerations to address when you telecommute. Unlike older children with whom you can negotiate, reason or bribe, pets are not always so cooperative. And while they won't scream like a baby, incessant barking or meowing while you're on the phone with colleagues or clients is not likely to enhance your image as a serious professional. Rather, it will reinforce misperceptions about telecommuting, distract you and your caller, and frustrate your pet if you continue to ignore those persistent pleas for attention.

Having a pet can have many positive benefits—companionship, exercise opportunities, etc. To help you enjoy the benefits of pet ownership while minimizing potential problems when you telecommute, advance planning is imperative. If you're just getting a dog, consider a puppy kindergarten class for you and your pet to instill good habits and establish roles (you ARE in charge and the pet needs to know this!). You might also benefit from reading books on pet care or talking with other telecommuters who also own pets. If you're just beginning your telecommuting experience, think about how you'll manage this with your pet.

- Do you have a telecommuting-friendly pet?

- Do you have another room to move the pet into while you're working? Or are you willing to spend the money to find a pet sitter (yes, there is such a thing as pet daycare!)?

- If it proves to be problematic, will you/can you give up telecommuting? Or are you willing to find a new home for your pet?

Those who telecommute with pets at home have found a few ways to make it work:

- Obviously, if you have a quiet pet and one that doesn't like to sleep on your desk or someplace that requires you constantly step over it, it's very comforting to have your pet with you during the workday. So, don't hesitate to do this if it makes you and your pet happy.

- If your pet occasionally is noisy (when the doorbell rings, a delivery truck stops by, etc.) you'll need to quickly hit the MUTE button on your phone. (A telecommuting friend of mine simply apologizes for the interruption of her "security alarm" when her dog barks.) Or you might be able to evoke complete silence immediately by having a plentiful supply of pet treats readily available.

- If your pet is unpredictably or constantly noisy, the pet has to go (to another room, to a pet sitter, or to another home). You may only need to relocate the pet if you have a critical phone call, a conference call, or some other task that requires focus and concentration on your part. Of course, your pet must be willing to stay outside your office without destroying the room or creating such a racket that it still hinders your work.

- If noisy pets continue to plague you, remember the numerous advantages of having fish (e.g., they're VERY quiet, fun to watch, and can contribute immensely to your meditative time).

TIP^2

Identify: Any ways that your pet compromises your ability to work effectively and efficiently.

Create: Solutions to any pet problems you have (or anticipate).

Decide: When and how you'll implement the solutions.

TRANSFER IT PROMPTLY TO IMPROVE PERFORMANCE

42 Resolve Disagreements Promptly

Making the transition to telecommuting can be a stressful and difficult process for everyone impacted by it. Expectations, roles, needs, demands, perceptions—these are all influenced by your telecommuting arrangement and can result in tension, anxiety, anger, resentment, and conflict.

In spite of establishing clear expectations and negotiating agreements (Tip 31), disagreements may arise. Whether you share your home with a stay-at-home spouse or someone who is a full-time employee commuting to a traditional workplace or a partner who also telecommutes (Tip 46), there are likely to be some points of conflict. It's wise to be alert to these conflicts and to address them quickly and effectively. This allows you to minimize the negative emotions and sources of stress that can undermine your telecommuting effectiveness and vital personal relationships.

When a conflict arises, deal with it promptly and proactively. This doesn't mean you should necessarily stop working to discuss the conflict "in the moment." Sometimes circumstances necessitate that you acknowledge the conflict situation and defer the discussion to resolve it. This is fine, provided you set a specific time to have the discussion and then *be sure* to follow through. One of my telecommuting colleagues occasionally runs into conflict with his wife regarding who is available to transport their young children to and from school or to extracurricular events. Since they both work and both have unexpected demands creep into their schedules, conflicts can arise unexpectedly. They talk "in the moment" about how to resolve the immediate problem, and they have a commitment to each other to follow-up later in the day or evening about how to avoid same problem again, how to be more flexible or creative the next time, etc.

Is your telecommuting causing any conflicts or lingering sources of stress between you and the people in your home? If so, or whenever a conflict does arise, be proactive about identifying the conflict and creating an opportunity to quickly work through it to a resolution. The resolution you reach is a function of the type of conflict and is dependent upon your unique situation. You may find that the solutions involve either more or less time together, establishment of clear boundaries or expectations, changed parameters regarding time and space, a shift in responsibilities, or increased flexibility. Whatever the resolution, it will be facilitated greatly and strengthened by the increased openness and communication you'll achieve with a positive process for resolving conflict.

TIP²

When discussing a problem or conflict, be prepared to:

☛ Stay calm (emotions can run high, so be conscious of remaining cool).

☛ Listen carefully and respond with empathy to concerns, feelings, frustrations.

☛ Ask for additional information regarding the problem.

☛ Reflect (repeat back) what you've heard to confirm you understand both the facts and the feelings expressed.

☛ Ask for input regarding ideas, suggestions, possible solutions.

☛ Share your own thoughts, perspective, feelings parameters, needs.

☛ Work together to discuss proposed solutions.

☛ Agree on action steps and any further discussion or follow-up required.

TRANSFER IT PROMPTLY TO IMPROVE PERFORMANCE

43 Accept the Guilt— and Move On

It seems sometimes that we've become so conditioned to feeling guilty that we've forgotten how to enjoy moments of delight without some angst about something. If only telecommuters had the perfectly balanced, blissful, unstressed and guilt-free life that nontelecommuters think we have! But, it's not likely. While you may be better off than when you spent 2½ hours of your life everyday commuting, the quest for balance and bliss is an ongoing one. So if you're contemplating or just beginning a telecommuting venture, don't expect a miracle. And if you've been at it for a while and are wondering why nirvana eludes you, take heart—you're not the only one, and it's probably not anything you're doing wrong.

In spite of admirable self-discipline, organization, focus, and commitment to balance, many telecommuters experience feelings of guilt, especially in connection with their children. Working at home should allow you to see more of your kids and participate more actively in their lives. It also makes you more vulnerable to their requests for your time and attention. For some telecommuters, this translates into a double-edged sword of guilt: feeling guilty when you're at home working and *not* spending time with the kids, AND feeling guilty when you are spending time with the kids or involved in their activities and you're *not* working. Well, let's fast-forward to the bottom line—you can't be in two places at once (or if you can, please e-mail me immediately with your secret!), and balancing the conflicting top priorities of work and family is just part of the equation (so we'll just have to deal with it).

One way to deal with it is to maintain, with constant vigilance, your commitment to boundaries between work and the rest of your life, as well as your commitment to limit any workaholic tendencies (Tip 6) you're prone to. Another technique is to interject a bit of perspective into your view of things. Ask yourself, when you feel that you've just subjected your child to the most disastrous disappointment, "Will this really matter 10 years from now?" Children are so resilient that sometimes a trauma you'll agonize over for hours won't bother them for more than 10 minutes. The perspective litmus test is also useful when you're psychologically gnashing your teeth over a decision to defer work to do something important with your family (accompany someone to the doctor's office, attend a program at your child's school, have an extended lunch with an elderly parent). I've always found it useful to consider these choices and decisions in light of "the grand cosmic scheme of things."

Realize that guilt is a natural response to some of the choices you make. But if you maintain a balanced perspective between the pressures of immediate demands and the long-term rewards of the choices you make, you're bound to find the wisdom to make choices that are right for what you value now and for what will keep you guilt-free down the road when you look back on your life.

TIP²

Think about decision points in your life that evoke feelings of guilt. Take some time to contemplate the values behind the feelings. Consider how to minimize guilt so you can move forward with the confidence that your choices are the best ones for now and for the future.

TRANSFER IT PROMPTLY TO IMPROVE PERFORMANCE

44 Answering Phones: Decide Who and How

Your telephone is a primary link between you and the rest of your business world. While your phone lines may also be used for fax, data, and video transmission, the voice contact you have with others is vital. Therefore, it's important for you to have well-established and communicated phone procedures. While a ringing phone has become quite a commonplace event in our everyday life, the ringing of your business phone should elicit a much more attentive and thoughtful response than usual.

It's likely that you'll want or be required to have a dedicated phone line for voice communication. For one of my corporate telecommuting stints, I had five separate lines installed (the phone company loved me!): 2 lines for voice, 1 for fax, 1 for the computer modem, and 1 ISDN line for videoconferencing. While you might not require this many lines, be sure to assess your needs and negotiate with your employer to secure an adequate number of business lines for your purposes. Once your business voice line is established, you'll need to think about where it rings and how it will be answered.

Ideally, your business line should be restricted to ringing in your home office, completely separate from your home telephone. Depending on your circumstances, you may want the flexibility to answer the business line in other parts of your home. This is fine, provided you can control who and how the phone is answered if you don't manage to grab it on the first ring. You may experience some difficulty with business calls coming into your home if you have young children just discovering the delights of answering the phone or teenagers who are convinced that every call simply must be for them. If either of these conditions is present in your home, consider doing the following:

- Do not let your business calls ring outside of your office, and do not let your children answer your office phone.

- Use voice mail, an answering machine, or an answering service to take messages when you can't answer your business phone yourself.

If you must have business calls follow you from your home office into other parts of your home:

- Install an extension of your business line in your home and locate it someplace where young children can't reach it (and teenagers know to never touch it).

- If available from your phone company, use an additional phone number with a special identifying ring on your home line so you can forward your business line to this number—and don't let your children answer the phone when this ring sounds.

- Forward your business calls to your cellular phone and keep the cell phone on your person at all times.

While some books about home-based offices provide guidelines for training family members to answer business calls and take messages professionally, this rarely is appropriate for corporate telecommuters. Unless your business is unique, your employer extremely flexible, and your clients graced with inordinate understanding, it's not likely that your callers really want to talk with anyone in your house other than you.

TIP[2]

Review your telephone situation to assess:

☎ How messages are recorded on your business phone line and any improvements you can make in this procedure.

☎ The opportunity your family has to answer your business calls and the appropriateness of this.

☎ The degree of access your calls have to you when you are not in
    your home office and any need to alter this.

TRANSFER IT PROMPTLY TO IMPROVE PERFORMANCE

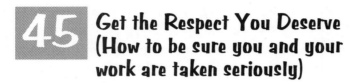

Get the Respect You Deserve (How to be sure you and your work are taken seriously)

Since many myths and misunderstandings still exist regarding the
life of a telecommuter, it's sometimes difficult for other people to
take you and your work seriously. The perception others have about
someone "at home" is that the person is not really or seriously working (since they perceive home is not a real or serious workplace).
The burden for achieving the regard, respect, and seriousness you'll
need rests squarely on your shoulders.

For you and your work to be taken seriously by others, *you* must
take yourself and your work seriously. All of your effort to focus your
energies, organize your work, plan your day, and monitor your
progress are major contributors to a self-perception of seriousness. It
also helps if you maintain established work hours—and be sure to let
everyone (immediate family, relatives, friends, neighbors) know
what those hours are. Additionally, it will help convey a sense of purpose and seriousness if you conduct yourself seriously (another good
reason to get out of your robe as soon as possible). In spite of these
efforts, some of the people in your world will feel compelled to
bother you. Oh, it's not that they (consciously) intend to sidetrack
you; they just might be unable to restrain themselves. So, you'll need
to arm yourself with a few weapons to keep these people (and their
inherent distractions) at bay:

- In addition to looking the part of the serious home-based professional, sound like it also. Always answer your phone (even
  the home line if you happen to answer it during work hours)
  with your name and/or your company name. This conveys the
  message that you're talking from your office and you don't have
  time for chit-chat.

- Always refer to your workplace as your *office*. ("I'll be in my office until 5:30, but I can return your call in the evening." "Why don't you call me at my office; the number is...") Referring to your workplace as *home* sends the wrong message and confuses people about your need to delineate between work and home.

- Be clear and assertive with people about your needs, time constraints, and work demands. ("I need to meet a deadline on a client project and can't talk now." "I've got a conference call waiting for me, so I'll have to talk with you later.")

- Make it clear to everyone who calls you, stops by, or rings your doorbell that you need to focus on your work during business hours and defer nonwork matters to nonwork times. ("I'm in the middle of writing a proposal and need to get it expressed out today. What's a good time for you to talk after work?")

- If you use a headset or have a portable phone handy, never answer the door without one of them attached to your ear—few things convey an urgent sense of "work in progress" as well as these.

- Does it go without saying? During work hours, absolutely avoid initiating any contact with neighbors or social interactions that are not essential. No one will understand why they can't simply reciprocate whenever the spirit moves them (which will always be at a time when you don't have or shouldn't have the time to spare).

Be alert to the temptation by your neighbors to take advantage of your availability. A telecommuter I know has been asked at various time to watch a neighbor's child, sign for an express package, give a key to a service technician, feed a neighbor's pet, water someone's plants while they were on vacation, and serve as a pick-up point for Girl Scout cookies. The accumulation of these intrusions on your time and focus will erode your productivity, increase your annoyance, and make you feel not very neighborly.

When the situation is approaching an emergency, it's probably appropriate to help. Recently, for example, my neighbor's children arrived home from school one day and found their door locked. So they rang my doorbell, and I wouldn't have thought of not welcoming them into my home to wait for their parents. Of course, right after I offered them milk and cookies, along with access to either the library or the television, I returned to my office to continue working.

Be reasonable about helping when the circumstances justify it.

However, when neighbors make intrusive or inappropriate requests for your help, let them know that you'll be busy at work (in a phone meeting, on a conference call, etc.) and won't be available. Otherwise, you'll become the local "drop-off/pick-up/central" as well as headquarters for neighborhood services, such as security watch and baby/house/pet/plant sitting.

TIP²

Review your approach to your work and evaluate how effectively you convey a sense of focus and professionalism to those around you. Consider how you might dress, act, and talk differently to communicate a strong *"WORK IN PROGRESS; DO NOT DISTURB!"* message. Select at least one thing you can change immediately with regard to how you handle nonwork visitors or phone calls that interfere with your work day.

TRANSFER IT PROMPTLY TO IMPROVE PERFORMANCE

46 The Happy Marriage/Partnership Guide to Office Sharing

Many of your traditional office-bound colleagues are fairly convinced that telecommuters enjoy the best the work world has to offer—a decent wage, minimal commuting, independence, etc. If you happen to also share your home office with a spouse or partner who telecommutes, you'll be the envy of just about everyone you know (except those people who can't imagine that much proximity to a loved one). True, sharing an office with a life partner has lots of advantages in terms of time together, awareness of the ups and downs you each experience, and involvement in the challenges and rewards of each other's work. That assumes, of course, that you happily and productively manage the shared office arrangement. There are lots of ways to transform this into a recipe for disaster. And the disastrous consequences are multiplied because of the impact not just on your work, but on your relationship, as well.

It all begins with the relationship, as with any partnership. If your relationship is shaky, it's not likely that telecommuting together will improve things. Rather, you'll probably experience added strain to the relationship and additional stress on your work that prevents you from being successful on either front. So, consider a shared telecommuting arrangement only if your relationship is strong and your ability to separate your relationship from your work is well honed.

On the foundation of a strong personal relationship, there are several steps you can take and agreements you should reach to establish a productive working relationship:

- If your office is an open work environment (like the cubes you tried to escape!), follow basic open office etiquette guidelines (e.g., don't use speaker phones, avoid loud talking, respect the designated space of others, maintain a not-too-slovenly work space, etc.).

- Position desks and work areas so that sound from equipment and voices moves in a direction opposite from each other's work space.

- Avoid "stream of consciousness" babbling; avoid interrupting with a thought, question, suggestion, or news flash unless you've asked permission to disrupt your partner's work or concentration.

- Respect not only each other's space but also equipment, supplies, tools, and resources. Ask permission for or have clear agreements regarding the use of things that belong to the other.

- Take great care to track expenses associated with any shared equipment or services (e.g., fax, computer, Internet, mail metering, etc.) so that reimbursements can be handled appropriately.

- Decide on phone procedures (who answers phones, how messages are to be handled, etc.).

- Take time out to be together when you can by sharing work breaks, lunch breaks, "erranding," success celebrations, mundane office chores (such as filing, cleaning, etc.).

Whenever possible, negotiate these issues (Tip 31) in advance and check periodically (Tip 47) to be sure that things are working well for both of you.

TIP²

When you're ready to discuss shared office issues, first check to see if it's a good time to interrupt your office/life partner. Schedule a meeting or a working lunch to discuss ways to more effectively work together. Think of one thing that you can suggest to improve the productivity of each of you.

T R A N S F E R   I T   P R O M P T L Y   T O   I M P R O V E   P E R F O R M A N C E

47 Schedule Periodic "How Goes It" Meetings

Your commitment to work well with your family may include a number of focused efforts:

- Set clear expectations with family and friends (Tip 31)
- Reach agreements and resolve conflicts (Tip 42).
- Make necessary arrangements for family care (Tips 35, 39).
- Manage the logistics of your home and office (Tips 13, 33).
- Make time to celebrate milestones together (Tip 32).

In spite of these efforts, there may be just a few bumps in the road you take to telecommuting bliss. Why? Mostly because of two things: all of this involves *people* and *change*. Since few things stay constant and people need continual attention and nurturing, be prepared to review, revise, revisit, and renegotiate regularly. I suggest doing this during regularly schedule "how goes it" meetings with your family.

Having a predetermined time to discuss problems, eliminate obstacles, resolve issues, etc. helps you avoid more highly charged, overly emotional "in the moment" discussions. While urgent matters may call for an impromptu discussion to resolve a problem, less critical, annoying, or nagging situations should be deferred to a designated time with a structured process for handling them. You'll find also that the little bumps and molehills along the way don't seem like such mountains to circumnavigate when people know there's a time, place, and way for charting a resolution to problems.

When to hold your "how goes it" meetings depends on several factors: how new you and your family are to telecommuting; you and your family's tolerance for stress, ambiguity, and delayed gratification; and the degree of change occurring within your family and your work demands. It's useful to establish the frequency for "how goes it" meetings during the early discussions with your family members when you establish expectations (Tip 31) and ask for their help as part of your team (Tip 32). It's helpful to also agree on the format for these meetings.

You might use an initial meeting with your family to propose the "how goes it" meeting concept as a way to channel issues for discussion. Discuss a timeframe and structure that addresses the concerns and needs of various family members. Don't forget to use effective dispute resolution skills (Tip 42) when handling concerns or discussing conflict.

TIP²

Use the following "how goes it" meeting guideline to keep lines of communication open and to minimize conflict situations:

- " Review solutions and agreements discussed during previous meetings or discussions and assess their effectiveness.
- " Ask for input regarding any new or unresolved problem areas.
- " Exchange ideas about things being handled successfully and discuss keys to success. Also share successes/good news regarding achievement of work goals.
- " Share any concerns, issues, obstacles you're experiencing and ask for input, improvement ideas, and proposed solutions.
- " Agree on action, next steps, and/or any follow-up required.
- " Confirm the date, time, and location of the next "how goes it" meeting.

TRANSFER IT PROMPTLY TO IMPROVE PERFORMANCE

Working Well with
Your Team

48 Establish a Rock-Solid Foundation of Trust

Underlying every successful relationship is trust. Without it, people become suspicious, noncommittal, uncaring, undermining and jaded—all of which leads to deteriorated and nonproductive relationships. This further leads to unpleasant work environments, disgruntled workers, frustrated customers, dejected leaders, and unprofitable organizations. So, while you're just one person in the whole intricate array of people and relationships in your organization, it's exceedingly wise for you to make trust-full relationships a major priority. As a telecommuter, establishing unwavering trust in relationships with colleagues and your boss is particularly vital, since distance and the absence of day-to-day interactions can create pressure on relationships that will erode trust.

The fundamental ingredients of trust in the working relationships that are critical to your success include reliability, consistency, and integrity. Knowing how these factors affect trust and how your behavior affects perceptions and beliefs is important to your success while telecommuting.

Reliability essentially means that people have confidence that you will honor the commitments you make. A good rule of thumb here: undercommit and overdeliver. So, don't make a promise on your voice mail greeting to return calls by the end of the day if you can't be certain you will. If you commit to attend on-site meetings or to participate in conference calls, show up. (Remember that you're not the only one who worries about being forgotten; people remote from you can begin to wonder if you remember them or care about their concerns if you don't follow through on your commitments to them.) Avoid not being available when you've scheduled time for a specific phone call or videoconference. Everyone gets unnerved if your essential availability and your ability to honor commitments is perceived as unreliable.

Trust is also strengthened by consistency. Be available to people on a consistent basis by establishing your home office work hours and maintaining those hours routinely. If you won't be in your office as scheduled, take steps to be accessible (Tip 52). Additionally, try to be consistent in your temperament and tone when speaking with people, responding to voice mail and e-mail, and participating within your team. Being unpredictable emotionally (a screaming maniac one day and happy-go-lucky the next) makes it very difficult for people to be comfortable with you, and trust will suffer.

Integrity is vital to trust, since it reflects how people perceive your ability to be honest in your dealings, truthful in your encounters, and respectful of the rights of others. While there's plenty of confusion, indirectness and hidden agendas in work relationships, it's important that you avoid these negative dynamics when you telecommute. Do this by remembering to:

- Be honest in everything you do. Once your honesty is compromised, trust is lost.

- Be truthful and forthright (without being obnoxious about it). People may not always like what you say or believe, but at least they won't have to wonder about it.

- Avoid sarcasm, joking, and teasing in your distance interactions. So much of what you say on voice mail, send in an e-mail, or blurt out in a conference call can be misinterpreted without you ever having the chance to know, respond, or recover.

- Maintain confidences so that you're not perceived as a "highly networked grand-central-station" of gossip or confidential information people have entrusted to you.

- Treat sensitive material appropriately. Don't send group broadcasts on voice mail or forward to the entire team an e-mail meant for your eyes only.

 TIP²

- Consider steps you can take to be more reliable and consistent.

- Look at your work habits, your team involvement, your interactions with colleagues; also think about any feedback you've received regarding any concerns about your availability and follow through on commitments.

- Identify three immediate steps you can take to improve your reliability.

TRANSFER IT PROMPTLY TO IMPROVE PERFORMANCE

Keep Your Boss Informed

"Out of sight, out of mind" is a major fear of telecommuters, and, depending upon the working style of your manager, it may be a bona fide fear. While you'll want to maintain visibility in the organization, keep your network active, and secure the necessary support of colleagues and subordinates, don't overlook the critical relationship between you and your boss. Don't be fooled by the expressions of envy from your friends and nontelecommuting associates who think lots of "space" between you and your boss is a dream come true. Too little contact with your boss can be very damaging to this critical relationship, so you'd be wise to overcommunicate whenever possible.

Telecommuting is facilitated greatly by the range of alternatives for communication (telephone, voice mail, e-mail, fax, groupware, etc.). These options in no way eliminate the effort and time still required to ensure effective communication in critical areas. With differing schedules, time zones, travel commitments, information needs, and communication styles, it's a real challenge to overcome the obstacles to effective communication with your boss.

Even with your best intentions, however, you may find that your boss is unreliable about keeping appointments or is sorely lacking on follow-through—all of which brings it squarely back to you. Regardless of the barriers, you have the responsibility and the greatest vested interest in relentlessly keeping your boss updated on your results, problems, opportunities, and need for her or his support. The "no surprises" theory is a good rule of thumb here: Never let your boss be surprised by anything about you or your work that you should or could have communicated promptly.

Be conscious of communicating with your boss daily—by e-mail, voice mail, page, or telephone. This keeps dialog active, even from a distance, and maintains your visibility on your boss's "radar screen." Ask yourself periodically if you feel your issues, challenges, problems, and achievements are visible enough to your boss. Also, are you clear about how much time your boss feels is appropriate for face-to-face and phone meeting time? If not, discuss and agree on this.

TIP²

Use interaction opportunities with your boss either to provide an update or seek input, guidance, or other assistance from your boss. Focus your communication so that your boss clearly understands:

1. What the topic is that you're addressing.
2. What the problem, need, or opportunity is.
3. The degree of urgency or seriousness the situation represents.
4. What action or input you need from your boss.
5. When that action or input is needed.

TRANSFER IT PROMPTLY TO IMPROVE PERFORMANCE

 Know and Nurture Your Team

The relationships and interdependencies you have with your formal team members (e.g., those co-workers with whom you work directly and/or who focus on the same projects, accounts, or functions that you do) are inherent in the structure of your organization and the processes whereby work is accomplished. The relationships certainly require nurturing, and efforts to strengthen them should be ongoing as your team develops and evolves. As a telecommuter, you need effective relationship-building, communication, and interaction skills in order to function effectively as a virtual team member. Also, as work processes change, marketplace pressures increase, and communication tools evolve, these relationships and interdependencies also reformulate. Beyond the scope of your formal team, however, there's likely to be an array of other colleagues who constitute your total virtual team. Identifying these colleagues and realizing their value to your attainment of goals is essential to your success.

Beyond the support staff that works with you directly, your success is contingent upon the work and commitment of any number of other resources that you may access throughout the organization. These might include:

- Billing/collection agents
- Editors/proofreaders
- Consultants
- Proposal developers
- Salespeople
- Shipping and receiving
- Audio-visual technicians
- Executives
- Computer systems specialists
- Maintenance staff
- Customer service representatives
- Graphic designers
- Installers
- Peers
- Managers
- Receptionists
- Library/information services
- Dispatchers
- Help-desk technicians
- Travel coordinators

The members of your broader team, while they might not be taken for granted, are often overlooked when considering who comprises your team. If you're typical, you have a long list of associates throughout your organization working with and for you. And especially in your telecommuting role, you're even more dependent on these resources and their commitment to your success. Knowing who they are and taking steps to recognize their efforts will be invaluable in ensuring their ongoing support (especially during the "crunch" times when you most need it).

Begin with a commitment on your part to stay connected to these remote but critical resources through simple efforts: a call, e-mail, page, or voice mail to thank someone for their help; a memo to someone's manager praising him or her for some extraordinary effort; nominating someone for an award for continued excellence in his or her work or attitude. Not forgetting who makes you successful will ensure that those people don't forget you when you're really counting on them.

TIP²

Identify:

3 Resources or associates who are not members of your formal team.

2 Specific things each of them has done or ways they help you that's critical to your success.

1 Action you can take now to recognize their effort in some appropriate way that communicates to them (and to others in the organization) how valuable they are to you and why their contributions are critical to your telecommuting success.

TRANSFER IT PROMPTLY TO IMPROVE PERFORMANCE

Stay in Touch with Co-Workers

With the time you invest each day in accomplishing your work; communicating with clients, partners, and your boss; addressing the technological and administrative issues critical to your work; and maintaining some semblance of balance in your life, it's very easy to find little or no time to stay connected with your co-workers. Certainly you'll communicate with them when it's essential to your work, but it's also important to stay in touch with co-workers for nontask purposes. This not only strengthens the foundation of your relationships, it also assures your co-workers that you're present (albeit in a virtual way!), available, and aware of them and their issues. It also helps to minimize any resentment (Tip 53) your nontelecommuting co-workers may feel toward you and your telecommuting work arrangement.

Don't expect your co-workers to necessarily take the initiative to keep in touch with you—they're busy, too! And you have the "out of sight, out of mind" deficit to overcome as well, so my strong suggestion is that you take responsibility for keeping these connections active. Don't hesitate to incorporate these initiatives into your daily task list, right along with the other key activities essential to your success. Otherwise, they will get lost in the flurry of your busy days. Here are some basic ways you can be sure that your co-workers won't forget you:

- Talk with them regularly by telephone. (Tip 52)

- Schedule face-to-face meetings periodically.

- Use every available minute when you're on-site in the main office to see and talk with coworkers. (Mingle over a cup of coffee, suggest a team lunch or work break, etc.)

- Try to attend social events (retirement parties, baby showers, promotion celebrations, etc.).

- If getting to your office doesn't involve a flight or a long commute, schedule meetings periodically in your home office with individual co-workers or your team.

- Use any other available technology (fax, e-mail, paging, video-conference, web conferences, etc.) to stay connected and visible.

- Volunteer for project teams or task forces that facilitate your involvement with co-workers.

- Rely on a trusted colleague or two to be your "ears" on the grapevine.

- Make a point to remember birthdays and acknowledge special accomplishments of your team members and associates.

 TIP²

✔ Review your schedule of meetings, trips to the corporate office, special company events, etc. to identify easy and natural opportunities you have to interact with co-workers.

✔ List the people you need to maintain a relationship with and different ways you can interact with them during these opportunities.

✔ Also add to your calendar specific steps you'll take to keep in touch with co-workers between opportunities for face-to-face interactions.

✔ Be sure you schedule at least two such actions each day and that you communicate with each key co-worker at least once every other week.

52 Be (Creatively) Accessible by Telephone

The demands of your job, pressures of your life, and distance between you and team members makes being accessible a triple challenge. But the sense that you *are* accessible, in spite of your telecommuting function, is vital to your success—especially if you are a team or project leader, supervisor, sales manager, account executive, or resident expert. No one doubts that live, real-time, face-to-face interactions generally are superior, but we don't live or work in an ideal world. So, you'll need to find creative ways to overcome barriers to your accessibility and to compensate for your physical absence.

The telephone is the primary tool you use for staying connected. While fax, e-mail, and videoconferencing can be useful supplements, many telecommuters still depend significantly on the telephone for communication—it's easy to use, generally reliable, more comfortable for some people than new modes of communication, and has superior quality (clear sound, no delay in transmission, etc.). Since people will use the phone as a key way to contact you, you'll want to be highly accessible via the telephone. Toward this end, keep these suggestions in mind:

☎ Have a second line, use call waiting, and/or have voice mail on your business line to minimize the calls you miss.

☎ Be diligent about returning calls quickly.

☎ Use call forwarding to ensure that your calls reach you when you're away from your office (Tip 91).

☎ Use caller ID to know when to interrupt another call or activity to respond to a critical caller.

Beyond voice-to-voice communication by telephone, you can be creatively accessible and visible in other ways:

• Use teleconferences, videoconferencing, and web conferencing to participate in meetings and attend presentations real-time— or even be a "virtual attendee" at a baby shower by asking to have a speaker phone available.

• Without sending unnecessary or annoying messages, be an avid user (by accessing these systems many times throughout the day) of e-mail, voice mail, and paging to accelerate communication and bolster your responsiveness.

- Encourage team members and co-workers to call you whenever they need your help or input, with your assurance (followed up by reality) that you'll be there or will return the call quickly.

- Have your home office business phone number added to the corporate speed-dial system so you are a mere few digits away!

 TIP²

Evaluate your accessibility by telephone (or ask some of your co-workers how easy it is to reach you for live communication). Identify three improvement steps you can take to improve your accessibility, and be sure to let your co-workers know about these new and easier ways to reach you.

TRANSFER IT PROMPTLY TO IMPROVE PERFORMANCE

53 Don't Ignore Those Who Resent You

If you are a trailblazer in your organization and an "early adopter" of the telecommuter workstyle, it shouldn't surprise you to encounter misperceptions about your work and your life. Even if you and your organization are fairly savvy with regard to telecommuting, you are likely to have some colleagues or co-workers who resent your non-traditional work arrangement. Depending on who these folks are, how critical they are to your success, how influential they are in the organization, and how effectively you handle situations, their impact can range from a mild annoyance to a serious undermining of your credibility and effectiveness. It's unwise to simply disregard resentment and assume it won't affect you or how you're perceived. Rather, you should be aware of it and try to eliminate it whenever possible.

You may become aware that someone is making comments about

your "cushy life" or suggesting that you're always inaccessible. I worked once with a fellow executive who consistently referred to me being "at home" when I wasn't on-site at corporate headquarters. (My loyal team members assertively corrected him by referring to my being "in her office in Pittsburgh" and asking if he needed to talk with me.) Of course, if there's any truth to the complaint that you're not accessible, you'll want to correct this situation immediately by being more responsive to voice mail, e-mail, and phone messages.

Letting people know in advance when you'll have limited accessibility due to travel, meetings, appointments away from the office, vacation, etc. also minimizes the frustration that can lead to resentment. In reality, you wouldn't always be accessible even if you worked on-site, but people tend to forget this and can be much less forgiving when you telecommute.

The most direct way to address resentment from co-workers is to confront it head-on. When you hear of persistent comments made by a key colleague or you think a co-worker is trying to erode your credibility or effectiveness, you can make great strides in eliminating this behavior by discussing it directly. Have a specific discussion with your co-worker about what you've seen or heard (being careful to not compromise confidences or create a problem for another co-worker) and discuss reasons for the resentful feelings. Listen and reflect what you hear; it's likely to be mostly emotional (anger about not also being able to telecommute, frustration about the stresses of commuting, etc.).

You might also learn that your co-worker perceives or actually experiences some additional work burden resulting from your telecommuting. If this is the case, explore ways to resolve the situation (Tip 63), particularly if an unfair burden has inadvertently been placed on the co-worker.

It's likely that any effort you make to understand the feelings of a co-worker (even if nothing changes with the circumstances) will pay huge dividends in how you are perceived by your colleagues. Being known as sensitive, concerned, empathetic, open to input and a good listener will never hurt you and is likely to minimize any barriers created by expressions of resentment, envy, frustration, or anger from your co-workers.

TIP²

☛ Identify any sources of existing or potential resentment among your colleagues and team members.

☛ Think about anything you're doing (or not doing) that might be contributing to their feelings.

☛ Focus on a critical relationship where resentment is a problem and schedule time to talk with that co-worker during your next opportunity to meet face-to-face.

☛ Discuss reasons for the co-worker's feelings, steps you both can take to improve any problems with work flow or load, and any other actions you can take to minimize the resentment.

TRANSFER IT PROMPTLY TO IMPROVE PERFORMANCE

 ## Network to Stay Visible and Informed

Networking usually is positioned as a critical activity for entrepreneurs and home-based business owners. While it's also seen as an important skill for anyone in business, networking cannot be overrated for telecommuters (unless, of course, it's done at the expense of achieving your goals). To the extent that you should manage your career almost as though it were an entrepreneurial venture (Tip 30), mastering the fine art of networking is certainly in your best interest.

Entrepreneurs who network effectively:

• Make it a point to meet as many people as they can.

• Create opportunities to be where other successful people are (or where potential prospects will be).

• Join organizations and participate in activities that keep them visible and involved in their field.

- Go out of their way to introduce themselves (i.e., work the room).

- Ask questions to get people talking about themselves (to make them comfortable and ensure that they remember you).

- Make sure people know their name, what they do, what they can do for them.

- Exchange business cards with their network contacts and keep good notes of conversations, potential opportunities, etc.

- Follow up periodically with contacts to keep their network viable, create opportunities to collaborate, exchange information, etc.

Maintaining active communication with your immediate and extended team, as well as networking more broadly within your organization, establishes vital links for you as a telecommuter. Constantly look for ways to do what successful entrepreneurs do:

- Meet lots of people and know people in other departments/divisions.

- Get involved in projects beyond the immediate scope of your job.

- Offer to help when your knowledge or expertise would be valuable to others.

- Keep in touch with people by briefly "checking in" or exchanging information.

Some telecommuters make a particular point to very actively communicate with others in the organization who are well-connected with the grapevine. To the extent that information and power go hand in hand, it never hurts to be in the know—and to be known.

 TIP²

Reevaluate your networking strategy and activity level. Look for and activate:

3 Ways you can get more involved in your organization and meet more people.

2 Networking contacts added to your daily call list.

1 Agreement with a reliable and well-connected on-site colleague who is willing to be your "eyes and ears" in the grapevine.

TRANSFER IT PROMPTLY TO IMPROVE PERFORMANCE

 ## Stay on Track for Promotions (and Other Good Deals)

It's difficult to overemphasize the importance of visibility when you telecommute. Isolation and fear of being overlooked for promotion are two of the biggest fears telecommuters typically report, and probably for good reason. Avoiding isolation is somewhat within your control, and there are clearly steps you can take to deal with this (Tip 26). Staying on track for promotions (or job rotations) holds some different challenges but is also manageable with a concerted effort and commitment on your part.

Before fretting over the promotion you might not get, it's a good idea to be sure you really want it. What will it involve (greater responsibility, increased travel, supervision of others, the need to give up telecommuting)? Will the rewards be worth it (corresponding increase in income, new and challenging work, exposure to other aspects of the organization, requisite experience or skills for a future promotion or job opportunity)? Since you are the ultimate manager of your career (Tip 30), it's vital that you ask the questions and find the answers. If you decide that moving up, sideways, or along in some other way is best for you, then lay out the track that train needs to move on. Here are some ways to help you on your journey:

- Staying visible and keeping in touch with colleagues (Tip 51) is essential to not being forgotten in the far-flung land of telecommuting.

- Go out of your way to find opportunities to be involved in projects, special assignments, task teams, etc. that will expose you to greater numbers of people and aspects of the organization.

- Schedule a career planning meeting with your manager to lay out your goals, review your plan, outline your strategy, ask for input, and obtain your manager's commitment to help you achieve your objective.

- Broaden your support network and involve more colleagues in your projects, sales efforts, proposals for innovation, etc.
- Take classes, seminars, and workshops that will broaden your skills, expand your knowledge, and introduce you to more people throughout the organization.
- Actively network throughout the organization (Tip 54), with particular emphasis on those people from whom you can learn a great deal, help on occasion, and benefit by knowing.
- Be known for treating people with respect, including the lower level support staff (talk about a network!).
- Most important, be known for getting results and consistently doing so with honesty, integrity, and regard for others.

 TIP²

Revisit your plan for the next career step. Reassess your plan in light of your true desires, your circumstances, the tradeoffs, and the payoffs. Consider any help or input you might benefit from and schedule meetings or activities to make that happen. Revise your plan as necessary.

TRANSFER IT PROMPTLY TO IMPROVE PERFORMANCE

56 Know When to Ask for Help

Chances are you're relatively self-sufficient and independent. Most telecommuters report these characteristics as areas of strength and contributors to their success at telecommuting. Sometimes, though, self-reliance can result in a tendency to manage everything yourself. One telecommuter I know was, by most standards, technologically proficient and not reluctant to handle computer-related problems, software upgrades, or equipment installation. However, the time these activities consumed was disproportionate to the benefit. Although she liked the challenge of handling the technological side of her office, she came to realize that calling the help desk more often and shipping her notebook computer to corporate for occasional upgrades and servicing were wiser investments of her time and effort.

Even if you don't consider yourself to have high control needs, your ability and desire to function independently can lead to an inordinate (and counterproductive) desire to get things done without the help of others. There are a few reasons to avoid this syndrome:

1. In spite of your many talents and skills, it's not likely you're really an expert at everything.

2. Some tasks and activities do not offer a reasonable "rate of return" on your investment of time and energy (that is, you can make more money or be more gainfully productive by focusing on other things).

3. Those around you (family, friends, colleagues) soon stop offering to help, since you appear uninterested in and unappreciative of their efforts to help you.

4. You will be perpetually tired, frustrated, behind schedule, and unable to make much of a dent in your endless TO DO list.

As a rule of thumb, you'll probably want to directly involve yourself in tasks and projects if:

- They directly relate to your work goals and/or impacts your primary source of income.

- Doing so capitalizes on areas of major strength that are unique to you.

- They are highly critical, visible, or time-urgent matters with serious implications for you, your organization, a key project, or a significant client.

- They involve an area in which you are truly an expert and you are the very kind of person people hire for the particular content knowledge you possess.

- Even if you didn't have to do them, they're such a source of enjoyment, you'd do them for a hobby.

Otherwise, get help!! Delegate (Tip 60), ask team members for

assistance, enlist your boss to help or track down additional resources, tap your network, access the services of suppliers, hire a
contractor, or look for ways your family might pitch in.

TIP²

Before embarking on tasks and projects you should ask others to do,
ask yourself:

? Do I need to do this myself?

? What's the impact of me not handling this personally?

? Is this a good investment of my time and energy?

? Is there someone else who could do this better, faster, easier,
  cheaper?

TRANSFER IT PROMPTLY TO IMPROVE PERFORMANCE

57 Master Effective (Virtual) Interaction Skills

Telecommuting will pose some unique challenges for you if face-to-
face interactions seem to be the only way to be truly effective. While
no one would dispute that "live" interactions usually are preferable,
these are fast becoming more of a luxury. Increases in mergers, ac-
quisitions, and global competition have resulted in a geographically
dispersed workforce and growing numbers of telecommuters for
many more organizations. As part of this trend, it's critical that you
become an expert in the essential communication skills for successful telecommuters.

While you lose some of the communication subtleties gleaned
from eye contact, body posture, gestures, and voice tone, you can
supplement virtual interactions in ways that minimize negative ef-
fects of "distance dialog." Regardless of the purpose and nature of
virtual interactions, there are some underlying keys to ensuring a
positive and productive outcome. Whenever you dialog at a distance,
remember to:

➢ LISTEN! Your ears are also your eyes whenever you're limited to audio communication. Without the benefit of seeing gestures, posture, facial expressions, etc., you must keep your ears fully attuned to the discussion and be alert to signs of disagreement, misunderstanding, ambivalence, noncommitment, etc.

➢ Confirm that your listening skills are effective by reflecting (repeating back) what you've heard and confirming that everyone involved has the same understanding of what's been said or agreed to. Summarize throughout the discussion and at the conclusion. If necessary, confirm agreements via e-mail, fax, project notes, or memos to minimize confusion later.

➢ Establish a clear purpose and desired outcome for every interaction. Make a habit of knowing and communicating at the outset why the interaction is occurring, why it's important, what the goal is, and how the goal will be accomplished. Verify understanding and agreement on these points.

➢ Avoid one-way "tell" monologues whenever possible by checking for understanding, asking for input, encouraging involvement and periodically assessing comfort levels with audio quality, pace, progress toward goal, etc.

➢ Eliminate distractions of any type that create communication barriers for you or your remote colleagues. (Remember that distance itself is a significant barrier for some people, so be sensitive to the needs of others.) Avoid background noise, snacking, unnecessary multi-tasking, and poor quality equipment if these distractions erode your concentration or your ability to be fully engaged in dialog.

TIP²

Establish a format for handling virtual interactions you're involved in. Include an outline for setting the agenda and note reminders for effective listening. Keep the guideline near your phone and visible (or easily accessible in your calendar book or phone directory) and begin using it whenever you "distance dialog" with colleagues.

TRANSFER IT PROMPTLY TO IMPROVE PERFORMANCE

58 Technology Talk: Keys to Communicating Without Speaking

Technology has advanced by leaps and bounds our ability to effectively communicate without a "live" interaction. Many experienced telecommuters have even come to realize (and enjoy) the advantages in efficiency derived from eliminating real-time communication whenever possible. Notwithstanding the disadvantages of virtual (remote) communication, the successful telecommuter effectively determines the types of communication that can occur without a "live" interaction (Tip 59), effectively utilizes appropriate virtual interaction skills (Tip 57) and effectively uses the technology available to:

- Save time.
- Broaden the scope of information conveyed.
- Expand the number of people included in the communication loop.
- Improve communication clarity.

Of course, all of these advantages can become disadvantages if the technology is misapplied or overused. To avoid having people hit the DELETE button the moment they hear you on voice mail or having your name on the DELETE ALL list in their unread e-mail message box, remember these few critical rules and points of etiquette in the world of "technology talk:"

- Use whatever technological option is considered appropriate for the culture of your organization and appropriate for the medium. For instance, don't use e-mail for quick schedule updates if people prefer that on voice mail. Avoid using e-mail for anything sensitive or confidential if having it forwarded without your permission (or saved to come back and haunt you!) is either possible or potentially problematic. Word of warning: Consider any e-mail you send essentially saved forever since it may travel through multiple servers that have backup files retained indefinitely.

- Plan or outline in advance your voice mail messages to ensure that they're to-the-point, succinct, and clear. Stipulate the number of topics you plan to cover and say early in the message if it will be a long one. Make the reply expectations and options clear and easy to follow. Use the same criteria for attaining brevity and clarity in your e-mail messages.

- When sending or responding to voice mail and e-mail messages, include only those people who need to know. Copy a plethora of groups, hit the "All Company" button, or press "REPLY ALL" only if the message is truly of interest to such a broad audience.

- Begin your messages with a brief statement of purpose, objective, and target audience. Anyone not interested or copied inadvertently can quickly delete the message.

- If the message is long, complicated, or has complex response options, review the message prior to sending it so you can edit appropriately to eliminate any confusion or redundancy. If a voice mail message you've recorded is confusing, rambling, or full of nonwords (e.g., ah, um, well, you-know), erase it and try again.

- If your e-mail system has the capability, use a preformatted signature stamp that automatically attaches to your messages when you hit the "Send" button. The stamp should include your name and contact information (phone, fax, voice mail numbers, e-mail address) so that recipients don't need to take time to find this information.

- Don't use your highly efficient technological talk options when the best alternative is really talking or meeting with someone "live." (Tip 59)

- Be sure that your voice mail greeting (on both the corporate e-mail system and your home office voice mail) is clear about when you'll be accessible "live" or when you'll be able to return the call. Follow through on your commitment to return calls within the promised timeframe. Also, if your voice mail system provides an option for callers to bypass your message, include instructions for doing so in the early part of your greeting.

- When leaving a voice mail message for someone who is unavailable to talk, specify the purpose, time, and date of your call; provide the information or pose the question you called about; provide information about when you'll be available to talk and/or when you can call back; and specify any deadline for a response.

- When fax is the best way to transmit your message or information, avoid sending an endless volume of pages. If the document is very long, consider using e-mail or express delivery. Also, be sure that the font size on your fax document is large enough to be legible by the receiver. (Send yourself a test fax to see what your machine transmits and bear in mind that some fax machines slightly reduce the size of print on the page.)

- To save yourself time, expand your handy-dandy phone list to include the following information for your contacts (especially those you communicate with regularly): telephone number, fax number, voice mail extension (and message bypass code), e-mail address, cellular phone number, and pager number.

- Review your voice-mail greeting and make any necessary revisions for it to be clearer or briefer.

- Create a format for e-mail messages that includes sections for purpose, background, key information, action required, and deadline.

- Explore the use of a signature stamp that is automatically included in your outgoing messages.

TRANSFER IT PROMPTLY TO IMPROVE PERFORMANCE

 ## Determine the Need for "Live" Interactions

Now that you've mastered the fine art of virtual interactions and have discovered the wonderful levels of efficiency you can achieve through the avid use of technology for communication, you'll need to counterbalance this with the occasional need for "live" interactions. Whether these be "live voice" (e.g., phone or videoconference)

or face-to-face interactions, some situations will warrant your investment of time, effort, and money to connect with people on a real-time basis. While there are no hard and fast rules about when you should get involved in a live interaction, it's clear that neither too much nor too little emphasis on real-time communication is a good idea.

Some telecommuters initially lean toward more live interactions than might be necessary. This can be caused by lack of judgment about what constitutes a bona fide need, by mixed signals within the organization about what's expected, or by the telecommuter's desire to see colleagues or fulfill social needs. Other telecommuters can become overly zealous about being efficient, using technology, and minimizing travel at the expense of other people or critical projects that demand more personal attention. Generally, you should seriously consider talking or meeting with someone directly if:

- A critical relationship (client, team, organizational) is affected.
- A major revenue-producing opportunity or project is impacted.
- A critical client recovery situation is involved.
- Your boss or team specifically has requested your physical presence.
- You're trying to persuade or influence a decision, direction, or strategy.
- The information to be discussed is highly complex, visual (and a web conference won't work), or confidential.
- The situation is particularly sensitive or could become highly emotional.
- You are establishing a new relationship or building rapport in a forming relationship.
- A new project is being kicked off and initial planning for scope, timelines, deadlines, etc. are being set.

Whether you meet face-to-face or have a live discussion depends upon the significance of factors such as those listed above, as well as your proximity to the meeting location, time and money available for travel, the comfort level others have with technology (some people still dislike speakerphones for meetings, while others can't imagine doing business without them), and the culture of the organization.

Like those who work in traditional settings, you will sometimes have schedule conflicts or other reasons why you can't talk or meet with people when necessary. In these cases, you need to balance priorities, make choices, communicate reasons, and explore alternatives and compromises. Bear in mind, however, that unlike your non-telecommuting counterparts, there may be slightly less tolerance for your lack of availability (particularly if it's perceived that you are somewhat consistently unavailable). Your commitments, limitations, and choices might be perfectly rational, but any residual resentment others feel about your ability to telecommute (Tip 53) may affect how they react when you're not available to them. My advice: Exercise caution in choosing to *not* talk or meet live, since the need for your presence (voice or physical) may very well exceed your need for efficiency. At the same time, think through your decision criteria in advance so you don't lose many of the benefits of telecommuting by constantly being pulled into live interactions and meetings better handled through technology.

 TIP²

- Review (or create) your decision criteria for determining when you initiate a live voice interaction and when you participate in face-to-face meetings.

- Discuss the criteria with your boss and other team members (by e-mail or during a regular update meeting) to verify agreement on general guidelines for making decisions about live interactions and meeting participation.

TRANSFER IT PROMPTLY TO IMPROVE PERFORMANCE

 **60 "Distance Delegation" that Delivers Results**

Unless you work in complete isolation, are an individual contributor with practically no interaction with anyone in your organization, or are such a "lone ranger" that you love handling even the most mundane of administrative tasks in your office, telecommuting will afford you inherent opportunities to delegate from a distance. More than likely, you'll find yourself needing to depend on the help of others (Tip 56) and benefiting tremendously from the use of appropriate delegation skills.

Delegating tasks and responsibilities can be an unnerving proposition for some people, especially those who like to be in control of things or on top of details. Telecommuters have the added dynamic of distance, resulting in the sense of even less control, more frustration, and elevated worrying. Distance delegation, however, doesn't need to be riskier or more haphazard if both the delegation AND the follow-up are handled properly.

When delegating responsibility or tasks to subordinates, team members, or staff members who do not report directly to you, use the following guidelines in handling the delegation discussion:

- Clearly explain the task or responsibility you're delegating and explain its importance to you, the organization, the client or project, etc.

- Ask for input, concerns, or feedback regarding the delegation assignment, as well as how and when it's to be completed.

- Discuss any issues and verify understanding of the requirements.

- Agree on follow-up actions, monitoring methods, "red flags" to signal that help is needed.

- Communicate your availability (how, when, where to reach you) to provide any necessary support or assistance and your appreciation for the help being provided.

Just as the "proof is in the pudding," the successful result of delegation is in the follow-up. It's imperative that your delegated assignments not be lost in a black hole; you have a responsibility to establish monitoring and follow-up methods and to exercise them at the designated times. While you might delegate interim reports as part of the assignment, you'll certainly want reminders to pop up on your calendar on the days reports are due.

Many of your technology options—such as voice mail, e-mail, fax, paging, etc.—are wonderfully efficient ways to monitor delegated work and receive updates on progress. How you track projects depends on your systems; use your computer-based calendar, your paper tickler file, a giant deskpad calendar, or a wall calendar that tracks work in progress. However you choose to track and follow-up is fine, as long as it works and you use it faithfully. It's also imperative that you be relentless about follow-up, or word will get out that your assignments really don't need to be completed on time since you're not likely to remember anyway. This is deadly to your effectiveness (not to mention your credibility), and makes delegation a veritable waste of time.

Review your project tracking method to ensure that it's an airtight way to avoid drowning in a sea of delegated tasks. Streamline your follow-up reminders by creating simple formats in which you easily can insert the project name and report due. Get in the habit of checking each day, as part of your daily planning, for any reports or updates due and fire off a reminder before the close of business that day.

TRANSFER IT PROMPTLY TO IMPROVE PERFORMANCE

Manage the Performance Management Process

One of the strongest barriers to telecommuting is the lingering perception by managers that it's impossible to know if people are really working if they're not on-site. Of course, these are the same managers who often have little measurable data to verify that on-site people are working. (There may also be a corresponding relationship to the widespread use of computer games and popularity of Internet surfing during business hours!) The bottom line is this: Managers don't know if on-site workers OR telecommuters are getting their jobs done unless a meaningful performance evaluation process is in place that measures more than "face time."

For a performance system to be worth the time, effort, money, and agony it inherently entails, it must:

- Be easy to use (people, after all, tend to avoid complex, cumbersome, and painful things).
- Establish clear goals that are measurable and attainable.
- Provide for frequent feedback (that doesn't consume inordinate amounts of time).

Ideally, performance appraisal systems should also be consistently used throughout the organization. But we don't often live in an ideal world, so my advice is:

- If you are a telecommuter and don't feel that your goals are clearly established and understood consistently between you and your manager, initiate a goal-setting discussion and drive the effort to negotiate clear goals, tracking methods, and review dates. Go a step further and try to pin down the relationship between attainment of your goals and increases in your compensation and/or other rewards.

- Document and copy your manager on the goals you've agreed to, as well as interim updates on progress toward your goals. Since goal setting, update, and review discussions may be done by telephone, it's critical that telecommuters clearly document these discussions and agreements. Tracking progress toward goals may involve using standard documents supplied by the company or self-designed formats or systems you create. Avoid complexity and redundant systems—use your monthly report data, your calendar system, or your project tracking reports to capture data that document your attainment of key results.

- If you manage other telecommuters, establish a consistent performance management system for your team. Schedule goal-setting meetings with each team member to set goals, measurement methods, review dates, and rewards. Document the agreements and manage the process.

Performance review systems tend to be like lots of those other best laid plans—they can often dissipate, lose steam, get out of focus, and drop off the "radar screen" of priorities. Whether you are a telecommuter or a telemanager, it is absolutely in your best interest to manage performance. Don't be intimidated by the complexity such an effort can entail. Yes, there are very structured, complicated, time-consuming ways to monitor and manage performance. On the other hand, a simple approach is better than nothing at all. And any telecommuter without some way to establish, monitor, and measure negotiated performance goals is at risk to:

- Lose or have no focus.

- Invest time and energy in lower priority goals.

- Fall short of expectations (which exist, whether they're articulated or not).

- Fail.

TIP²

Assess the status of your performance management process.

✔ Is there one?

✔ Are goals clearly defined and achievable?

✔ Does everyone understand and agree on the goals?

✔ Are tracking and measurement methods functional?

✔ Are rewards clearly established?

If you answered NO to any of these questions, schedule time to discuss your concerns and recommendations with your manager. Be prepared to propose goals, measurement methods, and rewards if these are not currently in place.

TRANSFER IT PROMPTLY TO IMPROVE PERFORMANCE

62 Reach Agreements that Foster Commitment and Collaboration

Setting clear agreements regarding accountabilities and commitments with your boss, your co-workers, and your support staff will help you avoid a plethora of difficult, unpleasant, and time-consuming problems. Without clear agreements, you run the risk of diminished work standards, missed deadlines, delayed shipments, lack of follow-through, disappointed customers, and increased stress and frustration on the part of everyone, as well as declines in your productivity and achievement of goals.

As is sometimes typical, however, it seems there's never enough time to take care of something properly at the beginning, while we find lots of time to invest in fixing it later. A major tenet of the quality movement is DO IT RIGHT THE FIRST TIME, and this is a good rule of thumb to follow relative to setting expectations and putting agreements in place with your colleagues. Since telecommuting also limits your ability to "tweak" agreements and processes via impromptu meetings and informal face-to-face discussions, you'll need to be more structured and determined about having clear agreements in place. Both your success and your peace of mind may depend upon it.

Aside from difficulty in finding time to hold agreement-setting discussions, there are other reasons we tend to overlook this. Often we simply assume that everyone has the same understanding, commitment, and objectives we do. There are endless ways people can interpret language, define roles, and reach different conclusions from the same data; not all of your understandings will be inherently shared by others. Commitment and motivation vary greatly among people, and your priorities may not be embraced enthusiastically by other people if you don't make the effort to enlist their support. Without the help and commitment of others, your own success is compromised. So make it your habit to establish clear agreements and ensure that everyone is conscious of the agreements and committed to working collaboratively to execute them. Whether you're meeting face-to-face or facilitating an agreement-setting discussion remotely, use this process to accomplish your objective:

✔ Clearly state the needs and expectations.

✔ Explain why they're important and the consequences of not meeting them.

✔ Describe how the agreement will look when it's operating as needed.

✔ Ask about issues, concerns, additional information.

✔ Listen, reflect, discuss, summarize periodically.

✔ Mutually agree to parameters, requirements, resolutions.

✔ Document the agreements and distribute to everyone impacted.

✔ Establish a follow-up time to review progress and revise the agreement as required.

TIP²

☛ Review your priorities and the factors critical to successfully achieving your key goals.

☛ Are there any areas of confusion, ambiguity, or wavering commitment relative to the support you need from others to achieve your goals?

☛ Correct these situations or establish clear agreements on new assignments by scheduling a discussion and using the process above.

TRANSFER IT PROMPTLY TO IMPROVE PERFORMANCE

63 Resolve Conflicts Effectively and Proactively

Conflicts are bound to arise in the course of your work with colleagues, co-workers, suppliers, and customers. The source of conflicts may range from differences in beliefs, perspective, work methods, and interpersonal style to feelings of anger or resentment regarding your telecommuting arrangement (Tip 53). Conflict situations also are exacerbated by stress associated with workloads, time constraints, resource limitations, and miscommunication. You're in a unique situation as a telecommuter to be somewhat of a lightning rod for conflict due to your remoteness from the workplace, as well as any negative feelings people may have about your ability to telecommute.

Sometimes conflict lurks around you and takes form in indirect ways: deadlines missed, follow-through overlooked, meetings held without your knowledge, commitments not honored to send requested information or supplies, and a whole host of other passive-aggressive behaviors. It often manifests itself in flip remarks or body language you might miss as a telecommuter UNLESS you stay very tuned in to what's happening in the main office. You can do this by staying well connected to your team (Tip 51), actively networking (Tip 54), and keeping your ear to the grapevine (or relying on someone else's ear). Also, fine-tune your listening skills, since your ears must "see" so much for you when you work remotely.

Since conflict usually exists and percolates before someone brings it to your attention (or things blow up at some unfortunate, high-pressure, and inappropriate time), I strongly advise taking the initiative to proactively address conflict situations. This allows you to control how and when the matter is addressed, strengthens your skills in resolution and mediation (important skills in our world!) and ensures that the conflict situation doesn't continue as a detriment to your own projects, accounts, and goals. Also, planning a discussion to resolve conflict makes for a much calmer environment and facilitates the necessary objectivity to reach a satisfactory resolution.

When you're fortunate enough to have the opportunity to be proactive about a conflict situation:

- Begin by outlining the concern or conflict.

- Whether you're in a proactive or reactive mode, handle the discussion by using the guide below.

- Remember to ask plenty of questions about the circumstances (e.g., What's happening? How is this impacting you? How is this affecting other people and their work?).

- Also ask questions about the feelings that have resulted (e.g., How are you feeling about this? What's your major concern? What are your biggest frustrations?).

TIP²

When you become aware of a conflict that's impacting your work or team productivity, move quickly to meet with the key players. Prior to the meeting, think about the solutions you'll propose and concerns/barriers you expect others to raise. Discuss the conflict by following this guide:

" Clarify the conflict, concern or disagreement.

" Listen and reflect; stay calm; summarize to confirm understanding.

" Encourage sharing of information, feelings, recommendations.

" Discuss proposed resolutions and agree on a solution.

" Summarize actions, commitments, follow-up.

" Document agreements and copy everyone impacted.

TRANSFER IT PROMPTLY TO IMPROVE PERFORMANCE

Master the Fundamentals of Productive Virtual Meetings

Meetings usually top the lists of things people hate most about their jobs (right behind cubicles and obnoxious co-workers!). There are few things other than meetings that create the illusion of involvement and productivity while wasting tremendous amounts of time, money, energy, and motivation. As a telecommuter, you're sometimes spared the burden of participating in boring and unnecessary meetings by virtue of your absence from the meeting location, although you also can be dragged into badly planned and poorly led meetings via a technological connection. Meetings—productive ones—are sometimes vital to your ability to activate project teams, generate creative solutions, and efficiently communicate with your team. Learning how to plan, lead, and participate in productive meetings, therefore, can serve you extremely well.

As much as people hate meetings, many organizational cultures encourage the scheduling of a meeting without much thought as to the real need for a live meeting. Sometimes this is done to perpetuate the sense of involvement, even if decisions actually are made by a subset of the meeting attendees and/or made outside of the meeting itself. If you get the urge to schedule a meeting, therefore, keep these reminders handy to help you evaluate the real need for a meeting:

• The first rule of productive meetings is to hold a meeting only if it's necessary and it's the best vehicle to accomplish the objective.

- Use e-mail, voice mail, intranet, or individual discussions if a larger group meeting isn't vital.

- Don't hesitate to hold a meeting if you really need the input of your team or a cross-functional group of associates (for things like project planning, project updates, strategy setting, and business planning).

- Don't overlook the basic components of an effective meeting: agenda, meeting leader, effective meeting management, etc.

As a telecommuter, you'll often need to combine the use of different technologies to facilitate productive meetings of geographical dispersed teams. Survey participants to determine the best way to get the agenda to them, use videoconferencing if a visual component is necessary, use conference calling if voice-to-voice is sufficient, combine Internet conferencing for graphics with a conference call for the audio link, etc. Remember, also, that introducing meeting participants to technology for meetings (Tip 65) may require a focused effort on technical training and procedural issues or basic etiquette for courtesy, offering input and asking questions. Once people are comfortable with the technology and their ability to use it (without looking foolish!), your virtual meeting productivity will be greatly enhanced.

TIP²

In preparing for the next regular meeting you have with your team, your boss, or a project team, implement or suggest ways to improve the likelihood of a productive meeting:

- Plan the agenda and distribute it in advance (via e-mail, intranet, fax, or voice mail, if necessary).

- Be clear about who's responsible for what (meeting leadership, time keeper, note taker).

- Have available the necessary equipment, handouts, resource documents, and contributors.

- Adhere to established times for starting, taking breaks, and ending the meeting.

▤ Schedule follow-up actions and future meetings before departing.

▤ Distribute meeting minutes promptly.

You might distribute this guideline to attendees in advance of the next meeting and ask for other ideas to improve meeting productivity. Be sure that responsibilities are clearly assigned and that meeting notes are distributed promptly. Suggest a way to use technology to save time and/or improve the productivity of future meetings.

TRANSFER IT PROMPTLY TO IMPROVE PERFORMANCE

Make Everyone Skilled and Comfortable in Virtual Meetings

Virtual meetings offer some unique challenges for both meeting leaders and meeting participants. While telecommuting, you'll find yourself participating in meetings remotely and connecting to the meeting via various types of technology. You have a responsibility to contribute and participate in a way that makes your participation valuable, justifies your investment of time, and helps other participants get the most from your contributions. Also, as a telecommuter (and sometimes as the only virtual participant in meetings), you may need to be a "champion" for effective skills and techniques necessary for successful virtual meetings.

Some people are initially uncomfortable with alternative technologies for conducting meetings. If they're not busily worrying about how they look on the videoconference screen, they're fretting about how to interject a question during a conference call. As a result:

☹ They tend to withdraw and say nothing.

☹ They completely forget you're at the other end of the phone line and start talking about a graphic on the screen only those in the meeting room can see.

☹ Everyone talks at once and you're totally confused about what's being said and who's saying it.

Before using technological applications for meetings, it's a good idea to formulate some guidelines and give people some hands-on experience with the equipment prior to any actual meetings. Some organizations are diligent about this and provide structured training available on a just-in-time or independent basis. (I can recall creating a mini training module for users of an early electronic blackboard system in the early 1980s. Everyone was more comfortable participating in actual meetings after a brief time of training and practice.)

When participating in a conference call, videoconference, Web conference, or any other kind of distance dialog involving a group of people, be sure to:

- Encourage everyone to introduce themselves at the beginning of the meeting and to identify themselves every time they speak (unless the video allows everyone to see clearly who's speaking or the group is a well-established one and voices are recognizable).

- Establish protocols for encouraging and simplifying involvement by all participants. The meeting leader should pause periodically to summarize and ask for questions, corrections, clarification, or suggestions. (During one of my corporate telecommuting jobs, we introduced videoconferencing and used it extensively for team meetings and executive meetings. Because of the audio delay, it was difficult to interrupt the conversation when multiple locations were connected. So we devised a system of small hand-held cards to hold up which visually prompted the meeting leader to pass the "floor" to the location holding up a card. We used visually appropriate cards to indicate the nature of the comment: question mark for questions; a light bulb for an idea or suggestion; a smiley face to indicate agreement with the discussion or proposal. We often used the smiley faces or just a visual "thumbs up" when a vote was needed, since communicating visually was easier than audio transmissions because of the delay and faster because we could see everyone's vote on the multi-frame screen.)

- Ensure that the use of any visual or graphic resources can be distributed "real-time" to everyone (via electronic white board, e-mail, intranet, Internet, fax, etc.).

- Everyone should be reminded to speak slowly, clearly, and in the direction of microphones or speakerphones. If you didn't hear something, ask that it be repeated. This reminds people of your "presence" and lets them know you're really interested in their comments.

TIP²

Review the various technology methods you use to "attend" meetings. What can you do to help the meetings be more effective, help others be more comfortable, and improve your own contributions and level of participation? Identify:

3 Problems you've experienced as a virtual meeting participant.

2 Advanced planning or meeting preparation steps you can take to eliminate these problems.

1 Action you can take during the next meeting to improve effectiveness of the meeting.

TRANSFER IT PROMPTLY TO IMPROVE PERFORMANCE

66 Just Say "No"

We're all surrounded with multiple opportunities to be distracted from our key focus areas. For many people, it's a daily challenge to avoid tasks, events, projects, as well as involvement in interesting and meaningful activities that will slowly erode energy and focus. Telecommuters face a unique challenge in this regard and one you should remain alert to. You're more vulnerable to requests or expectations from family, friends, and co-workers due to misperceptions about your availability.

When you telecommute, it's much easier for family members not only to interrupt you but to ask for your help, involvement, and input. After all, you're right there . . . it won't take *that* long . . . and isn't more time with your family one of the reasons you're a telecommuter?! Conversely, team members may think that telecommuting leaves you with lots of spare time on your hands or that you relish any opportunity for more involvement with your colleagues. While involvement—with both family and co-workers—is good, it's critical that you resist any temptation or pressure to be involved at the expense of your productivity. At the same time, you must be careful not to turn down every request for help, especially from co-workers whose help you may count on at times.

When faced with a request, demand, decision, or opportunity to involve yourself in anything that may detract from your major areas of focus, use the following screening guidelines to help you decide the best course of action:

- If the activity is insignificant in importance and unrelated to your priorities, just say "No!"
- If the request for your involvement results in time out of your office during established work hours, just say "No!"
- If the event or activity could occur at a more appropriate or convenient time, just say "No!"
- If it's a classic "nice to do" but not necessary or valuable to either your personal or professional objectives, just say "No!"
- If the request or demand is rooted in an intended guilt trip, just say "No!"
- If someone else is available to do it or can do it better than you, just say "No!"
- If the investment of your time has no payoff in terms of your current or future career goals and holds no intrinsic personal reward, just say "No!"
- If you'll be miserable the whole time you're doing it, just say "No!"
- If you'll hate yourself for agreeing to do it, just say "No!"

Remember to:

- Say "No!" gently and provide reasons why you can't help.
- Offer suggestions for alternative ways the requester can get what's needed.
- Propose a way you might be able to help with a portion of the request that won't be especially demanding of your time.

TIP²

➤ Assess the activities or projects you're involved in and consider which ones are appropriate, useful, or enjoyable.

➤ Reevaluate your willingness to continue involvement based on your assessment and determine whether any of them should be cleared off of your plate.

➤ Take steps now to begin uninvolving yourself in anything on the "cut" list.

➤ Promise yourself that in the future you'll commit to a more rigorous analysis considering pros/cons and have to/want to/need to considerations.

TRANSFER IT PROMPTLY TO IMPROVE PERFORMANCE

67 Work Productively With Co-Workers Who Share Your Home Office

Just when you think you've finally got an entire office to yourself now that you're telecommuting, some huge project or massive backlog of "administrivia" necessitates the addition of another associate—who needs to work hand-in-hand with you in your precious bubble of solitude! The advantages of getting the help you need might not appear to outweigh the disadvantages and potential difficulties of having someone else in your office (and your home). Or perhaps you really miss the interaction with co-workers, and having a real live person right in your office sounds great—until you find yourself unable to concentrate or become so distracted that your work begins to suffer. Having an on-site resource can be a real boost to your time, energy, and focus if you consider the implications and carefully craft a workable plan.

An on-site team member might be a part- or full-time employee and have a temporary or permanent assignment. To work most effectively with a co-worker who shares your home office:

- Anticipate the space, equipment, and resource requirements you'll each need and plan accordingly.

- Provide for convenient access to storage (for coat, hat, purse, etc.), a refrigerator, a coffee source, a restroom, etc.

- Negotiate clear work hours and any limitations on access to the office (especially if your co-worker must access the office through other parts of your home).

- Communicate or negotiate appropriate work standards and procedures. These will tend to be less formal than in a traditional office, but don't forget the bottom line—work still needs to get done right, fast, and on time.

- Establish a climate of open communication and agree to proactively address concerns or problems with the work environment, work flow, noise level, distractions, equipment, etc.

- As with other team members, take time to build rapport and establish a collaborative working relationship.

- Avoid an "all work/no fun" approach—take a lunch break together occasionally; celebrate a success or completion of a big project; or throw a little birthday or holiday party.

- Be ever-vigilant of the need to stay focused (while occasionally having fun), and avoid slipping into highly distracting activities like too much chatting (about sports, personal problems, main office gossip, etc.).

- Set in place a structured way to handle performance feedback and reviews to avoid only "in the moment" feedback. Discuss and document performance improvement plans when the situation warrants it. Keep your manager and any required human resources contact in the loop if you're moving toward any disciplinary or termination action.

- When an on-site co-worker resigns, completes the project or assignment, or otherwise terminates employment, be sure to retrieve keys to your house and office, keys to your mail box facility, and any company property in the person's possession (don't forget to change any security codes, passwords, or computer access).

If you need to recruit candidates, interview, and hire your on-site team member, keep these things in mind:

- For liability and insurance purposes, it's usually best if the person is employed by your employer rather than be paid directly by you.

- There may be ordinances or other restrictions in your community regarding a work site that includes employees other than the resident.

- If you need to advertise for candidates, place a "blind ad" or one with your company name and use a response box at the newspaper or the post office. Do not print your home address!

- It's wise to screen *very* carefully, including background checks and reference checks, since this person may have access to other parts of your home. Discuss security and legal issues with your human resources department, your telecommuting administrator, and/or your attorney.

- To minimize potential difficulties from hiring an unknown person, use your network to recruit referrals who come with personal recommendations.

- Be sure to clearly explain the home office situation to candidates, since some prospective employees would not be interested in such an arrangement.

TIP^2

Will there ever be a need for an additional team member to work in your home office? If so, how would you prepare for and handle that? If you currently have a co-worker sharing your office, what areas of difficulty exist? What are the significant areas of opportunity for improvement that would contribute to increased effectiveness and satisfaction by everyone involved?

TRANSFER IT PROMPTLY TO IMPROVE PERFORMANCE

Working Well with Your External Partners

68 Know Who Provides Your Critical Services and Support

You might feel utterly alone on some days, but the reality is that you're not—in more ways than you might have imagined. Of course, there's your family, friends, and your co-workers. There's also another critical network essential to your success: your external partners. Depending on your situation and the level of support you get from corporate services, a wide range of service providers may facilitate your ability to do your job. Here are examples of services you may need in the course of your work or to support you as a telecommuter:

- Accounting
- Bookkeeping
- Answering service
- Printing
- Personal services
- Administrative support
- Office management
- Research
- Mail/shipping
- Public relations/marketing
- Specialty subcontracting

- Conference/meeting management
- Tax preparation
- Graphic design
- Database management
- Equipment maintenance
- Temporary employment
- Security
- Office supplies/equipment
- Cleaning
- Internet service
- Interior designer/office planning

Some of these services may be supplied by corporate resources that constitute your extended team (Tip 50). Whenever this isn't the case, you may need to secure resources externally. Working well with your external partners can be as critical as the relationships you have with your team of co-workers. It's important to assess the degree to which external partners impact your ability to deliver the results you're paid to produce. Once that's clear in your mind, the importance of these relationships—how you establish, build, and nurture them—becomes more significant.

So, you're not an island after all. Therefore, knowing who helps you stay afloat makes for friendlier seas and allows you to be more productive and successful.

TIP²

Review your work, how you accomplish it, and who supports you. Identify:

➲ Whose help is vital.

➲ Where you do and do not have back-up options for critical functions.

➲ Any gaps in your current support system.

➲ An action plan to close the gap in at least two areas where your support system is insufficient.

TRANSFER IT PROMPTLY TO IMPROVE PERFORMANCE

69 Be Your Own Purchasing Manager

Whether or not you have the support of a corporate purchasing department, when you telecommute there are likely to be times you'll act as the local purchasing agent. At various points as a corporate telecommuter, I was responsible for the local acquisition of office supplies, printing services, administrative support, storage space, and meeting facilities, to name a few. My employers funded these expenditures through either expense reimbursement, a local checking account for business use, or a procurement credit card.

Your employer may have a sophisticated approach and standard for providing equipment and supplies to telecommuters. Often, however, telecommuters are left to their own devices to do this or work with corporate resources (information systems, accounting, accounts payable, administration, etc.) to determine what will best meet the needs of the individual telecommuter. Regardless of your circumstance in this regard, it helps you and your employer when you function with a "purchasing agent" mindset. Toward this end, it will be necessary that you:

• Know your real needs (Tip 83) and translate them into features and specifications for performance of equipment, services, and suppliers.

- Think seriously before purchasing and overloading your office with unnecessary, overly complex, feature-laden equipment. Be sure you'll need immediate access to it on a regular basis and the capabilities/features are justified by your daily needs and projected output. Otherwise, lease, rent, or subcontract for services.

- When considering the purchase of capital equipment, calculate the complete cost of acquisition and ownership; consider supplies, ongoing maintenance, service, insurance, and operator time.

- Evaluate the "return on investment" for major purchases in terms of the improvement you project in your efficiency and results.

- Whenever possible, request an on-site trial operation period for equipment that's expensive and/or highly critical to your work.

- Consider purchasing used furniture and equipment if it's in good condition, not technologically outdated, and acceptable to your employer if you're charging back the cost.

- Avoid single-source providers whenever possible unless the product or service is extremely unique.

- Be assertive about driving a bargain and asking vendors/suppliers to match or beat competitive prices or service offerings.

While you should avoid unnecessary or extravagant purchases, don't hesitate to purchase (or request approval for purchase) anything that will enhance your performance, improve your productivity, and fit comfortably in your office. Consider a few examples:

- If you've grown much more dependent on your notebook computer for days you travel or commute to the office, you may really benefit from having a docking station or port replicator to use in your home office.

- Don't buy an expensive, high-end copier if you have only occasional projects that require its features or your copy count per month is negligible. Instead, you may want to purchase a multi-function fax machine that can serve as a copier for your limited needs.

- Don't buy a postage meter if you use e-mail extensively or primarily require the services of package shippers and express delivery providers. Be sure to at least have, though, a postage scale and stamps in various denominations to use as needed.

- Don't waste money on a videoconference system if no one else in your company will have one. If audioconferencing is the primary mode of team communication in your organization, spend your money on a phone with all the bells and whistles, along with a top-quality headset.

TIP²

Think about the equipment resources in your office:

$ Are there any that don't have high enough usage levels to justify keeping them?

$ Should you purchase anything you're currently leasing?

Regarding services you currently buy:

$ Are there any services (printing, copying, document production) you currently buy at such volume that it's cost-justifiable to purchase equipment and bring the capability in-house? (Can your office support that?)

$ Are there any services you're currently purchasing that should be re-bid by multiple vendors to be sure you're getting the best price and service?

TRANSFER IT PROMPTLY TO IMPROVE PERFORMANCE

70 Select Service Providers that Meet Your Criteria

Articulating your needs for equipment and services has payoff both initially and over time. Of course, your needs may change as your telecommuting job changes, your workload increases, or your office expands. But if you establish the good habit of assessing and documenting your needs, it's easier to adjust as changes occur. This is critical to matching those needs with the providers best suited to meet your criteria.

Aside from the fundamentals of service excellence (quality work, delivered on time, at a competitive price, etc.), telecommuters should consider other criteria that may reflect individual needs and situations:

- Proximity to your home office.
- Free delivery or courier service.
- Ability to purchase in bulk (with a discount) or smaller quantities (if your storage space is limited) without paying a premium.
- Corporate or commercial discounts.
- Online support (for ordering, technical support, customer service).
- 24-hour technical support.
- On-site service/maintenance.
- Compatibility with your software and computer systems.
- Ability to bill your employer directly (or offer suitable payment terms).
- Extended hours of operation.
- Quick turnaround/response time.
- Multiple access options (e.g., phone, fax, e-mail).
- Equipment replacement or loan during service outages.
- Flexibility to handle rush projects (assuming you're not *always* in a rush!).
- Willingness to meet or beat competitive pricing.
- Friendly, service-oriented attitude.
- Positive "can do" attitude.

There may be other criteria unique to your needs; these will get you started and help you formulate your own criteria for working with suppliers that best meet your needs. Without clear criteria, you're bound to experience disappointment, frustration, wasted cost, and lost time. And it won't be the supplier that necessarily is to blame.

List several services that you purchase from suppliers. Identify the most critical one and list the specific criteria you have for the supplier of that service. Are your needs being met? If not, why not? Decide whether you may need to either:

➤ Have an expectation-setting discussion (Tip 71) with the supplier.

➤ Communicate your needs, timetable for improvement, and consequences (Tip 73).

➤ Request competitive bids for the work and reevaluate your vendor choice.

TRANSFER IT PROMPTLY TO IMPROVE PERFORMANCE

71 Set Service Expectations and Get Your Desired Results

Before you can set expectations for a service provider, you must have your needs clearly defined and know specifically the results you're looking for (Tip 71). This may include specifications regarding timeliness, material quality, adherence to established procedures, service orientation and skills, or equipment output levels. With clear criteria, you can begin by identifying potential resources. Use business listings, phone directories, referrals from your network, the chamber of commerce, or the Better Business Bureau to create a pool of potential suppliers. Since having clear criteria without viable vendors is like having a great job description without qualified candidates, screen suppliers the way you screen candidates for employment:

• Relevant experience

• Capability and expertise to perform the required work

• Motivation and interest in the type of work

• Affordability

- Availability.

Most suppliers appreciate having a clear understanding of the service or product you're expecting them to deliver. Printers like seeing a mock-up of a print job; cellular phone companies need to know your projected usage in terms of calling minutes per month and range of call locations; and writers want to know how you want people to feel or respond after reading their copy. If you run across a supplier that doesn't seem appreciative of your specificity, or worse, tries to tell you what you want, consider it a stroke of luck to get this red flag early, and don't waste any time before finding another supplier. Unless projects are extremely routine, it's usually a good idea to combine your written specifications with a "live" discussion. This is true especially for suppliers that are new to you. Circumstances might not allow you to meet face-to-face, but a voice-to-voice meeting allows you to:

- Review the printed specifications or written instructions.
- Describe in greater detail the purpose, need, and importance for the deliverables.
- Describe in detail the outcome, output, or performance standards you're expecting.
- Discuss any questions, suggestions, or adjustments to specifications agreed upon based on input from the supplier.
- Agree on interim checkpoints and deadlines to monitor progress and quality.
- Review the job contract (if applicable) and stipulate how executed copies should be handled.
- Secure a verbal commitment to the expectations and required deliverables.
- Agree on consequences for missing deadlines or compromising other quality standards.

It's also useful to help the supplier by providing information regarding your availability (phone numbers, pager number) or access to other resources (your assistant, a co-worker). This allows for questions to be answered or direction provided throughout the project and helps the supplier avoid unnecessary delays in completing your work. Having backup options and alternative ways to clarify expectations and needs is especially important for projects that are critical, complex, or time urgent.

TIP^2

✔ Review your supplier criteria and service specifications for a critical service you're currently outsourcing.

✔ If all aspects of the relationships and the delivered results are satisfactory, ensure that you're applying the same level of specificity in expectations to other outsourced projects.

✔ If not, clarify your criteria and expectations, prepare written specifications, and schedule a meeting with the supplier to establish expectations, requirements, and consequences.

TRANSFER IT PROMPTLY TO IMPROVE PERFORMANCE

72 Negotiate Deadlines and Details

Depending upon the nature and volume of your subcontracted work, you may have a wide range of details involved and more than one deadline to manage. Since telecommuters function somewhat like entrepreneurs in terms of independence from many corporate support services, you may secure contracted services in areas such as photocopying, administrative support, telemarketing, printing, or technical services. Negotiating the terms for these services is an additional responsibility you may have as a telecommuter that your central office colleagues don't need to handle for themselves.

Because you can't assume that service providers, even very experienced and competent ones, will inherently know what you want and need, it's critical that you be clear about expectations (Tip 71). As part of that process, there will be times that you'll need to be assertive about deadlines, costs, and quality standards. This is true especially if your needs are different from what the supplier typically provides to customers. With deadlines, for example, you should not hesitate to ask for a shorter turnaround time if you really need it sooner than the supplier projects. You can ask for suggestions from the supplier on ways you can make it easier (cleaner copies, different formatting, samples, prototypes supplied earlier, etc.) for the delivery date to be earlier. Although you can always find another supplier (someone else probably would love to have your business!) if there's significant resistance to meeting your needs, sometimes you'll want or need to negotiate on sticky issues like deadlines and more demanding deliverable details. When this is the case, remember to:

- Provide additional information about what's needed and why it's important.
- Listen to the supplier's concerns, barriers, and suggestions.
- Discuss options, alternatives, and compromises that balance conflicting needs.
- Offer and request flexibility.
- Agree on a solution and review details (e.g., deadlines, checkpoints, revised specifications, nonperformance penalties).
- Be certain that agreements are reflected in the contract or documented another way.

Beyond agreeing to clear specifications, deliverables, and deadlines, you'll need to negotiate penalties (Tip 73) for nonperformance. These should be tied to key milestone dates and/or quality standards for deliverables and are best negotiated along with all other project details.

TIP²

When preparing for the next supplier discussion you'll need to have regarding the assignment of a project:

- ✔ Consider what you'll need to provide in terms of written specifications.
- ✔ Plan the discussion by outlining the content you'll cover and the process you'll use.
- ✔ Be certain that your needs and expectations are clear and that you can define deliverable requirements in detail.
- ✔ Anticipate any areas of barrier or conflict in your negotiations with the supplier and be prepared to demonstrate and request flexibility and to propose alternatives that meet your key needs.

73 Establish Consequences for Unsatisfactory Service Performance

Many of your major equipment purchases will involve preestablished warranty terms with optional extended warranty or service contracts. You can negotiate occasionally with individual suppliers for more favorable terms relative to service. These might include a lower cost for the service contract, supplemental extended warranty at no charge, free loaned equipment during downtime for repair or maintenance, free shipping, and no charge for on-site service calls. As an individual telecommuter, you're likely to have some difficulty driving much of a harder bargain in these situations because you don't represent a major purchasing source to the supplier. This is true especially when dealing with superstores or major suppliers. However, if you're buying from a local source that caters to small businesses, you may have better luck. Of course, you may pay slightly more, but if you can negotiate some of the benefits and service features vital to a telecommuter who's highly dependent on equipment reliability, you may be better off.

You're likely to have more opportunities to negotiate the terms of delivery for services you receive from suppliers, vendors, and contractors. When establishing service requirements and performance expectations, you'll want to also include terms that protect you if the promised service is not delivered. For example, if you contract with a package and shipping outlet to ship product samples or to fulfill an order, your contract might provide for express delivery at the shipper's expense if a shipping deadline is missed. Penalties for performance below standards can be a huge incentive to a supplier to avoid anything short of meeting your requirements. You should, therefore, consider appropriate penalties attached to critical deadlines, quality standards, and deliverables essential to your ability to meet the expectations your customers, employer, or co-workers have of you. Penalties for nonperformance may include:

- Reduced payment on the current contract.

- Additional labor or product supplied at no charge for future contracts.

- Loss of performance bonuses attached to measurable results or deadline compliance.

- Free loans of replacement equipment.
- Free labor for service or maintenance when response to trouble calls are longer than agreed to.
- Discontinued use of the service provider for future work.

When possible, attach specific incentives and penalties to definitive project milestones or quantifiable delivery points. Keep rewards in mind when negotiating terms, since attractive incentives are often a more powerful inducement than penalties. Either way, you improve your odds of obtaining the performance you need and the results you're counting on.

 TIP²

☺ Identify a service you're receiving currently that isn't completely satisfactory.

☺ Clearly articulate where there are deviations from the required performance standards and what satisfactory levels of performance would involve.

☺ Consider ways to alter your service agreement with the provider so there are clear rewards for compliance and consequences for performance below targets.

☺ Choose at least two key deliverable measures on which to focus your action and discussion with the supplier.

TRANSFER IT PROMPTLY TO IMPROVE PERFORMANCE

 Get It In Writing

Your efforts to negotiate favorable terms, establish rewards or penalties, and provide for contingencies may be in vain if the agreements are limited to a discussion and verbal assent. Beyond that, a handshake is a nice touch but may not be terribly useful when you're trying to enforce terms of your agreement later on. As a telecommuter, you're not likely to negotiate service contracts that are highly complex, critical, or involve significant amounts of money. If you do, however, be sure to secure the support of your corporate legal office or a local attorney who specializes in contract law (not necessarily the same attorney that handled your will, your divorce, or a contested accident claim).

While our society has become somewhat litigious, it's wise to know when you do or do not need a formal document to secure an agreement for services. I worked once with two entrepreneurs who insisted that a contract was unnecessary for a project they were doing because their contact at a major publishing firm had made a verbal agreement and sealed the deal with a handshake. These two entrepreneurs idealistically believed that their contact was "good for his word" and the deal was solid. Well, as you might suspect, circumstances changed in ownership of the publishing firm, the contact seemed to more or less disappear, and the deal vanished into the same thin air in which it was struck.

Written agreements need not be jargon-filled, legalistic tomes that require an excessive number of billable hours from an attorney—unless, of course, the situation is complex, the stakes are high, or the contract is vital to your work. In this case, by all means, get the help of an attorney. If the agreements you want to document are simple, straightforward, and do not involve major financial implications, you can summarize your verbal agreements in the form of a letter, memo to the file, or a simple contract.

When greater formality or legal protection is wise, there are a number of software programs and other resources available that allow you to create agreements by simply plugging in the relevant information (names, dates, types of services, specific agreements, etc.) and attaching things like order forms, purchase orders and similar supporting documents. Agreements such as service contracts, personal guarantees, leases, service warranties, rejection of goods, etc., can be created using templates and then reviewed by an attorney to ensure they're properly worded, complete and legally binding. If you're contracting for legal services and execute a number of simple contracts, you may be able to save money by preparing a draft contract using a template and then hire an attorney to review and approve it. When I use this process with my attorney, it's very efficient since I know the details of the contract terms and save time by not having my attorney deal with them, and it's cost effective since I use my attorney's expertise in a very limited and targeted way.

In most cases, it's unlikely you'll need to take legal action against someone over a dispute covered by a written agreement. More typically, having the agreement itself will be a major inducement for delivery of the service or goods as stipulated in the agreement. Further, even a simple memo or letter documenting your discussion and agreements with a service provider can serve to clarify details and eliminate confusion later when the specifics may be a bit fuzzy to everyone.

Review the services you purchase from suppliers and the verbal service agreements you've made. Which of these involves enough importance, complexity, and dependence to justify a written agreement that will afford you greater protection? Discuss these situations with your manager, your legal counsel, your attorney or a business advisor. Determine which situations could benefit from a simple agreement letter and take steps to complete these. If more formal contracts or agreements are required, access the appropriate legal resources to execute whatever type of agreement is necessary to protect you, your employer, and your work.

TIP[2]

Using whatever method of documentation (e.g., contract, letter, e-mail, etc.) is appropriate, whenever you need to establish a service agreement, be sure to include language that clearly specifies:

➤ Who will perform the work and what, if any, assignment to others can be made.

➤ What products or services will be delivered and how the service is to be performed.

➤ What milestones of time or quantifiable output will signify compliance.

➤ How payment relates to milestones, deadlines, quality compliance.

➤ How performance incentives and penalties will be determined.

Review your existing service agreements against this template and determine where changes would be advisable.

75 Know When to Outsource

Expecting to do everything yourself when you telecommute is unrealistic. Trying to do everything yourself is undermining—to your success, your sanity, and your productivity. Let's face it, you're:

- Good at some things, lousy at others.
- Enjoy some things, hate others.
- Only one person (with only two hands, 24 hours in a day, and limits to your personal energy).

Besides the fundamental reality of your preferences and limits, there are some tasks you certainly *can* do but *shouldn't* do since your time is better invested in more productive, focused, revenue-generating or goal-oriented work. So, when determining what to outsource, ask yourself:

- Are you capable of doing this? Does it capitalize on your expertise, play to your strengths, and minimize your weaknesses? For example, if you're employed as a software engineer and need to upgrade some software on your computer, you're probably the best person for the job. On the other hand, if you're a marketing writer and need to install the same upgrade, it might be the right time to call your computer consultant.

- Will you enjoy doing this? Will you find the task to be challenging, energizing, or useful in developing your skills? If you're intrigued by the intricacies of the tax code and would rather wade through a tax return than do a 5,000-piece jigsaw puzzle, you won't want to bother hiring a tax preparer. However, if the thought of tackling your tax return raises your blood pressure or brings on feelings of depression, don't even consider burdening yourself with the expectation of preparing your own tax return—invest your time in other important tasks critical to your work or personal priorities.

- Can you, indeed, accomplish this on your own? Is there enough time in your day, space in your office, or physical and emotional energy in your life to tackle this? In spite of being the best person to do something and having a strong interest in it, you may simply not have enough time to complete it and meet the deadline without help.

When the situation warrants it, don't hesitate to get the help you need. If you're not sure it's cost-justified, calculate your hourly rate (annual salary + commission + bonuses + benefits ÷ 2040 = your actual hourly rate). With this in mind, you may realize how foolish it is for you to undertake some tasks that can be outsourced at a more reasonable cost. Use this information to make the case for your employer to pick up the costs of support services that are necessary to your work but counterproductive for you to complete personally. Even without your employer's funding, you may determine that outsourcing of some services is a good investment of your own funds.

 TIP²

Reevaluate the tasks you handle personally in addition to the major focus of your work. Do any of these involve work that:

- ☹ You struggle with due to skill deficiency?
- ☹ You loathe to do and avoid like the plague (creating a backlog that frustrates you incessantly)?
- ☹ Is consistently done during peak times when you are perpetually overwhelmed, behind schedule, and missing deadlines?
- ☹ Is routine, mundane, time-consuming, and not directly related to your goals and your critical results? Or someone else is better suited to handle?

Target areas where outsourced services can help you be more focused, productive, and less frustrated in achieving your key goals. Take steps now to identify options and resources for outsourcing.

TRANSFER IT PROMPTLY TO IMPROVE PERFORMANCE

76 Establish a Partner Mindset and Relationship

The most productive way for telecommuters to approach relationships with service providers is with a partnership mindset. While the relationship isn't a traditional partnership in that the parties are not co-owners or principals, each has an investment in the relationship. And although you "call the shots" since you're the buyer, thinking like a partner gives you a frame of reference to see your vendors, suppliers, and contractors as key members of your broader support team. Further, you're in a better position to work with them in ways that facilitate achieving superior results.

Thinking like a partner in your supplier relationships promotes the establishment of a long-term relationship mindset and fosters behaviors and attitudes that nurture this. The last thing you have time for as a telecommuter is searching continually for and experimenting with new service providers. It's in your best interest to have long-term relationships with established providers who understand your needs, support your standards, and are committed to delivering quality results for you.

While you might not invest the energy and time to build partner relationships with all of your service providers, doing so with those who are most vital to your success will have significant payoff. For example, the consultant who supplies computer support for your office and functions as your local help desk can be pivotal to your ability to function if you're highly computer-dependent. Getting a quick response to pleas for help is more likely if the consultant feels valued, understands your needs, knows what's expected, and is rewarded for performance "above and beyond." Also, "breaking in" a new computer consultant could be distracting, time-consuming, and costly—it's better to take proper care of the good one you have.

You have a critical role in building a strong alliance of key service providers. Without a committed and enlightened approach to this, you will experience turnover, disappointment, and frustration with your pool of key service providers. To ensure the development and retention of committed and competent suppliers, be sure to:

- Clearly establish your expectations, priorities, and requirements (Tip 70, Tip 71)—they can't "hit the bull's eye" if you haven't told them where it is.

- Be available to offer guidance, coaching, support, and clarity to help suppliers help you— remember the GIGO Theory (Garbage In/Garbage Out). Suppliers depend on you for clear instructions, specific measurements, sample products, photos, color swatches, material samples, prototypes, and legible hand-writing.

- Be firm in your demands, expectations, and consequences *and* fair in all of your dealings with service providers— insisting that a printing deadline, for example, be met is reasonable un-less you don't honor your commitment to produce masters or disks on time.

- Be proactive and direct in addressing conflict—when there's a problem with performance or a disagreement about a billing matter, don't delay or be evasive in discussing the issue and ne-gotiating a resolution.

- Always treat people with respect—being pushy, obnoxious, or condescending does not elicit any real or long-standing commit-ment to your success.

- Pay for services in a timely manner—service providers seem to appreciate this (just as you enjoy receiving your paycheck as promised).

TIP²

- What steps can you take to strengthen the relationship and be a better partner with one of your key service providers?

- What areas of difficulty exist in the relationship now (from your perspective)? What might the supplier's answer be to this ques-tion? (Hint: Don't guess; ask the supplier.)

- Decide on a plan to foster a stronger partnership with key ser-vice providers and target one or two critical providers to focus on for first steps. Schedule time to meet soon with your most vital supplier to get the ball rolling.

77 Treat People As People

Something as basic as treating people with respect and courtesy can get lost amid the pressure generated by work demands, family demands, and feelings of frustration and isolation telecommuters sometimes experience. This can be true especially in handling situations with suppliers where performance is below your expectations and you're feeling completely exasperated by the need to deal with the situation, by the time it's robbing from your work, and by the anxiety caused by the resulting compromise in your own ability to hit performance targets. Anticipating that there will be points where the pressure mounts, the conflicts abound, and your patience runs thin also will help you anticipate how to handle your interactions with service providers in those circumstances, as well as during your day-to-day interactions with suppliers and contractors.

Treating people as people is fairly basic (and calls to mind another maxim from Mom): Treat people the way you'd like to be treated. While the concept is simple, execution in the moment can be a challenge when dealing with service providers. Everyone can recall fairly readily some recent or amazing "service from hell" experience:

- Delivery service that fails to get materials to your client on time.
- Express service that extends the concept of "overnight" to multiple overnights.
- A major printing job done on the wrong paper, bound incorrectly, or cut wrong.
- Phone service that's intermittent at best.
- Technical help desk support that is always backlogged and rarely helpful or pleasant.
- Luggage that took a much longer trip than you did.

When we're paying for a service and it's delivered poorly or with an abysmal attitude, we are tempted to lose our manners and move toward major ranting and raving behaviors. Once this happens, of course, tempers flare, defenses go up, everyone gets entrenched, and nothing good can happen. While your anger, frustration, and disappointment might be completely justified, it won't make the service provider feel any more inclined to find a resolution—and it's likely you still need the provider's help and cooperation to solve the problem.

Additionally, how we treat service providers on a routine basis provides the foundation for working through more stressful times. In your work with and interactions with your key external partners, remember to:

- Treat service providers as valued members of your team with unique skills, abilities, and services critical to your success—remember them for holidays, send flowers or a fruit basket when their work was essential to you finishing a big project or closing a major sale, send a gift certificate for lunch or dinner (or have a plaque engraved) to mark a significant milestone such as "5 years of great service."

- Thank vendors and suppliers for ongoing good work and tell them specifically why their work is important to you and how they make it possible for you to be effective—give a verbal acknowledgment, a letter, a gift from the trip you won for outstanding sales results, or a plaque they can display in their place of business.

- Avoid rude, demeaning, or verbally abusive treatment—this is unacceptable business behavior and should never be used, especially if others are present and you embarrass everyone involved (yourself, in particular).

- Look for ways to reward performance (Tip 78) and show your appreciation, especially when someone goes that extra step for you—add a bonus to the next payment you make to them, agree to send a letter to your network promoting their services, or send a gift basket or unique gift from a specialty store.

- Ask for suggestions from your suppliers and show that you value their input by following their advice whenever appropriate—check with them during the planning of a project for input about ways to streamline the process or improve the end result, consult with them on subjective variables like color, layout, typeface, etc.

TIP²

Decide how you can acknowledge the effort and good work consistently delivered by one of your key service providers. Send a note, a fax, an e-mail, or plan to personally call or stop by to say specifically how the service you receive helps you do your job, makes your life easier, or contributes to your success. Make a point to look for opportunities to do this with all your key service providers during the next few months.

TRANSFER IT PROMPTLY TO IMPROVE PERFORMANCE

Reward Good Work

The number of creative and meaningful ways to reward the efforts and results of your service providers is endless, limited only by your imagination (or your budget). Often a simple and sincere "Thank you" is far more than service providers expect or typically receive, so praise (which is essentially free to you) can be more appreciated than gifts or other tangible rewards. Assuming you're a telecommuter with a network of critical service providers, minimal time to take from your work, and a limited budget for things such as supplier rewards, consider these alternatives for letting your suppliers know how much you value their contributions to your success:

- Just say, "Thanks!"
- Take your supplier to lunch.
- Create your own "You Done Good" award certificate and send it when appropriate (just don't overuse it).
- Send a letter (or fax or e-mail) explaining what was done well and why it was important.
- Have a plaque inscribed with the vendor's name and a "Service Excellence" notation.

- Have breakfast or lunch catered for the suppliers' staff.
- Send a gift unique to the supplier's line of work or personal interests.
- Ask your manager or CEO to send a letter of thanks.
- Deliver a tray of cookies or bag of bagels and cream cheese (with a balloon and note or sign with a thank-you message).
- Send flowers or a fruit basket or a balloon bouquet (or a tin of cookies, popcorn, or mixed nuts).
- Bring a gift back from vacation or an award trip you earned (especially if the superb service is related to work done in your absence).
- Present a gift certificate for dinner at a great restaurant, for a round of golf, or for a massage.
- Offer to promote the supplier's services within your network.
- If you know the supplier enjoys it, give a bottle of champagne or case of beer.
- Give tickets to a ball game, the theater, the zoo, a museum, the circus.
- Give phone calling cards or discount buying cards at a local retail store.
- Present a monogrammed shirt, briefcase, golf club covers, sweat suit.
- Offer to help or contribute some of your expertise to the supplier.
- Send Thanksgiving cards instead of holiday cards and include a note saying why you're so thankful for the supplier.
- If you know or can find out the supplier's birthday, send a card or fax or a bouquet of balloons.
- Present a trophy when the effort was herculean.
- Give an airline ticket earned with your frequent flyer miles.
- Present a book (autographed by the author is always nice) or books on tape, when more suitable.
- Give gifts of electronic items, office equipment, or jewelry when you know it will be valued and appreciated.

TIP²

Someone you know deserves a reward. Decide what's appropriate and take steps now to have it sent or presented as soon as possible.

TRANSFER IT PROMPTLY TO IMPROVE PERFORMANCE

79 Bartering for Best Results

Bartering, or the exchange of services, is generally a lost art and not one that most telecommuters consider in accessing services for a reasonable investment. But if your funds are limited, you have valuable skills to exchange, and your network of associates and suppliers is extensive, bartering may be a reasonable alternative for you. Let's say you're a marketing specialist who needs the services of a local printer, a computer consultant, and mail house. Each of these businesses may very well need the services of a marketing specialist, creating an opportunity for the cash-free exchange of services through bartering.

Before entering into a bartering arrangement, determine the fair market value for your skills and services and be sure to price your time and deliverables accordingly. Bartering does not mean someone gets a huge bargain by accessing the services of someone at a ridiculously low value. Rather, it's a fair exchange of needs for skills that is mutually beneficial to both parties. Because both parties realize a good value without incurring direct costs, it allows you to obtain services you might otherwise not be able to afford. Since there may be tax considerations if you participate in a bartered exchange of services, don't forget to check with your tax advisor about how to handle the reporting of services rendered and received.

You can find bartering opportunities by searching your network, as well as professional associations and civic groups you belong to. Other ways to uncover barter potential include:

- List your skills on your business card.
- Offer bartered services on a small flyer you can give to people at meetings.
- Post an offer on your web site.
- Send a mailing or e-mail announcement to suppliers, associates, friends, and colleagues.
- If your skills are relevant to their needs, expand your network to include start-up businesses and home-based businesses.
- Join or create a barter network.

Even though bartering is not a cash-based transaction, it should still be negotiated in a way that provides structure and specificity to the arrangement. And, as with other agreements you make for services, be sure to put your barter deal in writing (Tip 74). This ensures that everyone is clear about who will provide what deliverables in exchange for which services. Additionally, a written agreement will help you track the value of your time, as well as the value of services received.

While bartering may not be a major source of contracted services and support for your needs as a telecommuter, it should not be overlooked as an alternative. Think about bartering when you have a limited budget, pressing needs and something of value to offer to someone in a similar situation; bartering can be used very cost- and time-effectively by telecommuters.

TIP²

What skills and abilities would you be able to trade in a barter? What service needs do you have that aren't being addressed due to budgetary or time constraints? What sources are available to you in your network of contacts and resources to locate a potential barter opportunity that can meet your needs? What initial steps can you take to establish areas of bartered services?

TRANSFER IT PROMPTLY TO IMPROVE PERFORMANCE

80 Network Your Partner Network

Once you build a wide and reliable network of external partners who are your trusted service providers, you can capitalize on and strengthen this network by:

- Providing referrals within your service network.

- Connecting your service network contacts to your broader network of associates and colleagues.

- Tapping your external partner network for information about resources and services you may need.

- Depending upon your line of work, possibly tapping your external partner network for business prospects and sales leads.

You're in a unique position to provide referrals to your external partners regarding the other service providers you use. If, for example, you learn that your computer consultant is suffering from an office (or life) in a complete state of chaos, it helps both the computer consultant and the organization consultant you've worked with if you suggest to each of them that they should talk or meet. Your computer consultant will trust your first-hand referral and appreciate your interest in her or his success, while the organization consultant will be grateful for the prospective business opportunity and the regard you have for the value of the services you were provided. When you serve as a "clearinghouse" of information, connections, and contacts, you enhance the value of your external partner network and provide a cost-free reward (Tip 78) to your suppliers of excellent service.

Another way to reinforce and reward your supplier network is to connect these external partners to your business and professional network. Look for opportunities for your suppliers such as: print the membership directory for your professional association, make presentations to civic groups, provide meeting planning services for your trade association, provide telemarketing services to your peers, obtain a low-cost ad in a civic association newsletter. Connecting your supplier partners with your network contacts in mutually beneficial ways can be highly valued by your partners, a useful service to your contacts, and helpful to you in strengthening the loyalty your partners feel to you.

Your partner network also can help you by providing information and referrals for other services and products you need. When you need to purchase a new printer, for example, ask your local printing partner, your administrative service partner, and your mail drop/quick print partner; all probably have a wide range of experience with multiple pieces of equipment and can help you assess the best option for your needs. Or when you need bookkeeping services, a referral from your tax preparer is a more viable option than responding to a listing in the yellow pages.

While you might leverage your partner network for business leads, this would be useful only if your business is targeted to the types of products and services used by businesses. In this case, you might selectively pursue leads or barter (Tip 79) for prospects within your partner network. In the spirit of partnership, of course, you'd want to offer to provide corresponding business leads for your partners. Your service partner network can be a rich source of information, referrals, resources, and potential business. Knowing how to mine your partner network can be productive for you, your partners, and your entire business network.

TIP²

☞ Look throughout your external partner network for opportunities to help your service providers connect with each other and with your extended network.

☞ How can you access information and opportunity within your partner network that can make your work more productive, cost-effective, and successful?

☞ Identify at least one opportunity to help one of your key service partners, and one opportunity to benefit from your partner network.

☞ Take steps to quickly act on these opportunities by making a call, sending an e-mail, or scheduling a meeting.

81 Follow-Up for Best Results

As a telecommuter, you are a prime candidate for developing absolutely superb follow-up skills. Since you need to work with and through so many other people—colleagues, vendors, co-workers, suppliers, team members, contractors, managers—to accomplish your goals, expert follow-up skills can be essential to your ultimate success. When you hone these skills for use, especially with your external partners, it conveys a sense of significance to their work, communicates its importance to you, and clearly establishes a standard of excellence for the way in which you manage and value your work.

Well-planned and consistent follow-up behavior is not a license to micro-manage. Nothing will frustrate and demoralize your external partners faster than excessive hands-on management from you that feels and looks like high-control interference in their work. Rather, your project planning should establish clear expectations (Tip 71) regarding milestones and checkpoints. Your role is to use these checkpoints as guideposts for your follow-up. Doing so should ensure (provided the project planning is sound) that you have adequate opportunity to monitor progress toward goals without overburdening yourself with the minutiae of a project or task. For example, checking in with a program developer who's designing a training program for you is useful if you do so at key milestones such as:

- Review of key learning outcomes that serve as the program mandate.
- Review of the design document that establishes the program blueprint.
- Review of first draft learner materials, leader materials, and video scripts.
- On-site observation and support during video shoots.
- Review of off-line video segments and final draft of print materials.

Calling the program developer daily would be unnecessary, distracting, and certainly annoying. It's more productive for everyone involved to have key checkpoints agreed to in advance and to establish contingency plans for discussing problems or seeking clarity during the interim between checkpoints.

With key milestones and checkpoints agreed to, along with the agreement that follow-up is part of the plan, you should focus your effort on adhering to the follow-up plan and making your follow-up activities appropriate. Use your calendar, a tickler system, or a computerized project management system to make your follow-ups as scheduled. Even if the supplier is scheduled to deliver a draft document to you by a specified time, it's your responsibility to monitor whether it's received and to follow up with a reminder about it if it's not received. Otherwise, without your evident management of follow-up milestones, the seriousness of deadlines is called into question—and this bodes badly for the outcome of the project, contract, or assignment.

Your follow-up may include a number of methods for monitoring the status of delegated work or projects in process:

- Regular update meetings included in the project plan
- Periodic project status reports
- Conference calls
- Face-to-face meetings
- E-mail
- Voice mail
- Fax
- Videoconferences

However you manage the follow-up on projects, assignments, delegated work, team efforts, or action steps agreed to by your manager, it's essential that you manage your own ability to adhere to follow-up schedules and commitments. Being vigilant about this is particularly critical for you as a telecommuter, since you will often be remote from those doing the actual work, and you're not in a position to use less formal methods of "How goes it?" discussions over the water cooler. With a firm follow-up plan and schedule, you will feel more relaxed and confident about goals being achieved, and your service partners will appreciate knowing the structure and timing of checkpoints.

TIP²

Evaluate the follow-up plan on a major project, assignment, contract, or account:

☑ Does everyone know when checkpoints occur?

☑ Is the information to be provided at key points detailed in the project plan?

☑ ARE YOU CONFIDENT THAT WORK WILL BE DELIVERED AS YOU ENVISION IT?

If you answered "No" to any of these questions, send a fax, e-mail, or voice mail now to the service provider and schedule a meeting or phone conference to renegotiate milestones and checkpoints. Be sure that your time and task management system includes all the dates and follow-up points you need to manage and execute.

TRANSFER IT PROMPTLY TO IMPROVE PERFORMANCE

 ## Get the Most Out of Business and Professional Associations

Association membership can be extremely beneficial to telecommuters. Your memberships in business, professional, trade, industry, and civic groups can help you feel less isolated and more connected to people on both a business and a personal level. Associations also are good resources for information about trends, regulations, and dynamics affecting your business. Further, your involvement in business and professional groups can be a real boon to your networking efforts.

Like everything else, though, you get advantages out of your association memberships in fairly direct proportion to the effort you put into them. Joining associations for the sole purpose of accessing the mailing list for prospecting purposes is likely to have limited pay-

off. Rather, you can maximize the benefits of association membership and multiply your networking dividends by:

- Becoming active (e.g., attend meetings, at a minimum) in targeted associations (those that hold the greatest interest, rele-
  vance, and reward in terms of your work and industry).

- Accepting a leadership role in the association (e.g., hold elected
  office, chair a committee, convene a meeting, coordinate a conference or workshop).

- Forming a special interest group that focuses on your industry,
  on your area of expertise, or on telecommuting.

- Volunteering for a special project (such as coordination of a na-
  tionally sponsored teleconference with a satellite link in your
  city) or a high-visibility assignment (such as editor of the
  monthly newsletter).

- Volunteer to host a regular association meeting or present the
  program for a special workshop or seminar where you can share
  some unique knowledge, skill, or experience you have that
  would be of interest to other association members.

- Co-sponsor or co-present a workshop or seminar with one of
  your key external service partners to showcase a unique project
  or major effort you tackled together to achieve superior results
  (for example, a major client project you were involved in that
  required extraordinary response from one of your package design vendors—describing the need, the urgency, the collabora-
  tion, and the strategy to accomplish the work on time, on
  budget, and to the complete satisfaction of your client could be
  an intriguing case study to members of your association).

Any of these levels of involvement in an association will help you
feel more active and connected, be more visible, expand your network of contacts, and derive much greater value from the investment
of time and money you make in your membership. Connecting your
association network with your external partner network has, therefore, greater advantage to each of them and helps you leverage the
goodwill you've built across both networks.

TIP²

→ If you have been procrastinating on joining a valuable business, trade, or professional association, call or e-mail them now to process your membership application.

→ Otherwise, identify the most valuable association you currently belong to and list three ways you might become more involved to increase the value of membership to you and your business.

→ Take steps now to move forward on one of the ways you listed; make a call, jot a note, send an e-mail to move the idea to action.

TRANSFER IT PROMPTLY TO IMPROVE PERFORMANCE

Working Well with
Tools and Technology

83 Assess Your Real Needs and Choose the Best Technology for You

If you love technology, are exceedingly comfortable with the occasional ambiguity of computer use, and can't imagine an electronic gadget that would intimidate you, you're likely to embrace the notion of acquiring and integrating technology into your office and your work. If, on the other hand, you telecommute for reasons other than the love of technology (or, as a former colleague referred to himself, you're a "techno-twit"), the whole technological realm may annoy, frustrate, or depress you. It's unlikely you can telecommute successfully without it, so you're wise to find ways to see technology as your friend and learn how to be comfortable with technological equipment and products.

My advice is to read, ask questions, try out products in the store, search the Web, have a fellow telecommuter show you her or his techno-tools, field-test products, experiment with different equipment at business service centers, and get into a "hands-on" mode whenever possible. (After all, it's not like dabbling in a chemistry lab; there's little chance anything will blow up in a way that causes major damage!) To avoid being overwhelmed by the constantly changing array of choices, features, options, interfaces, and gadgets that bombard (and perhaps offend) your sensibilities whenever you need to select a technological product, it's a good idea to first carefully determine your needs and define the specific requirements you have in terms of size, output, capability, compatibility, etc. Consider the:

- 💻 Tasks you need to accomplish.

- 💻 Tools required to complete those tasks.

- 💻 Skills you have and will need to appropriately use the equipment you choose.

Of course, cost is usually a factor to be considered as well. What you must or would be willing to invest, however, should be determined by the overlap between these three factors relative to your personal use of the equipment and how it integrates into your work and your office.

Approach decisions regarding the selection and purchase of equipment by following this process:

✔ Define how you will use the equipment and the specific performance requirements to meet your needs. For example:

- Will you need your computer for word processing, spreadsheets, fax capability, graphic design, data analysis, database management, planning/scheduling, project management, etc.?

- Will your fax machine have a dedicated line, high-volume demand? Will you need to retain fax documents and require plain paper?

- What are your copying requirements in terms of volume, speed, size?

✔ Research the options designed to meet your needs. Don't forget to:

- Discuss your detailed specifications with a knowledgeable sales associate.

- Survey your external network to learn about equipment that's working well for colleagues and suppliers.

- Access information and assistance from corporate computer support resources.

- Check with co-workers and peers who also telecommute to learn about equipment they use satisfactorily.

✔ Test, retest, and field-test your options. It doesn't hurt to:

- Experiment with equipment in the store.

- Visit the office of a friend or colleague to try out his or her equipment.

- Ask for a trial period during which you use the equipment in your office and can return it if you're not completely satisfied (get this promise in writing).

✔ Make a final decision to purchase only if you've had a chance to "road test" the equipment and/or it can be returned (usually within 30 days) with no problem. Don't forget to:

- Use the equipment as much as possible and as soon as possible for various tasks. If you're counting on your fax to also function as a copier and scanner, test these functions fully.

- Return anything that falls short of your expectations, doesn't work well within your office, is difficult for you to use, or is uncomfortable in any way.

A final, but important, note about the technology and equipment that support your work as a telecommuter: Taking the time and making the effort to clearly articulate your needs will help you get the best resources. And when it comes to technological resources, don't settle for anything short of the best match of equipment to your needs. Shortchanging yourself on technology is a ticket to short-changing yourself on success.

TIP²

-⊕ Prepare a "spec sheet" for a piece of equipment you need to acquire that will allow you to telecommute more effectively or efficiently.

-⊕ Define your needs clearly in terms of how you will use the equipment, the level of usage you project, how it needs to work with your existing technology, any constraints (such as size, weight, power supply) within your office.

-⊕ Use your specifications to guide your review of options, evaluation of need versus capability, consideration of safety factors, and assessment of price versus payoff.

TRANSFER IT PROMPTLY TO IMPROVE PERFORMANCE

 # Know Your Backup Options (Before a Crisis Occurs)

In deciding what equipment you need to support your telecommuting arrangement, you'll typically plan for ideal operating conditions (your computer functions properly, the fax machine just keeps humming, your printer is not hopelessly jammed, and your phone service is uninterrupted). Life being what it is at times, however, it's also useful to consider what backup options you may need to continue being productive even when your equipment fails you (because it will, you know!).

This is where having a "Chicken Little" mindset is not a bad idea. Imagine that the sky is falling . . . or worse—WHAT IF your computer crashes?

- Do you have a spare computer easily accessible that you can switch to? Does it give you access to the key capabilities and software you need, including Internet and e-mail connections? (In a real pinch, you might borrow the computer from your kids!)

- Is there an external option you can access fairly quickly (a nearby business center, your local quick-print, a computer rental outlet)?

WHAT IF your printer goes haywire?

- Do you have a spare printer that's handy, loaded with the critical fonts you'll need, and capable of printing what you might need? (That 7-year old laser printer collecting dust in the closet might still produce dynamite word processed images but give you an uncooperative ERROR message if you ask it to print a spreadsheet.)

- Does your fax machine have multi-function capability and compatibility with your computer to serve as your backup printer?

- Can you save your urgent documents on disk and race to a neighbor's house or local business service center to access a printer? Is the service center available during the hours you may be having a crisis?

WHAT IF your phone service is disconnected by a careless driver six blocks away who wipes out a utility pole?

- While you might miss incoming calls during the phone down time, do you have a cellular phone readily available (and spare batteries always charged) to let your key co-workers, project associates, or clients know to call you on your cell phone? You also can use your cell phone to check voice mail while your land lines are out of service and to make any outgoing calls that will keep you productive and connected until phone service is reestablished.

WHAT IF your e-mail capability disappears (due to a problem with your software, the corporate network, or some server in between)?

- First, you (almost) cry.

- Second, pat yourself on the back for being prepared with an alternative. You may rarely access the Internet through your AOL account (or another Internet service you have for your kids), but it may be a critical resource for exchanging files and messages if your corporate e-mail and/or Internet services take an extended vacation.

- As a last resort, request that the sender (who's insisting that you read her or his e-mail ASAP) print and fax it to you on your reliable fax machine.

WHAT IF your fax machine goes on the blink?

- Here's a good reason to hang on to that relic of a fax machine with that annoying thermal paper on a continuous roll. If it still works, it might come in real handy if the power supply in your new one gets fried.

- Are you familiar with and easily able to set up your computer to send and receive faxes? Interestingly, this is a capability many computers have and some computer operators never master (probably the same people who don't know how to program their VCR). Quickly configuring your computer (or a spare computer) to both send and receive faxes can be a lifesaver for you.

- Can you divert any critical faxes to a local business service center? This would likely involve a commute for you to send and receive faxes, but it's better than being fax deprived!

Multi-function fax machines offer flexibility and can provide great back-up options in a telecommuting office, provided you have other primary equipment options. However, if you rely solely on your multi-function fax machine for faxing, printing, copying, and scanning, you're in a boatload of trouble if these multi-functions become nonfunctioning.

You get the idea—think ahead, consider your options, ask lots of WHAT IF questions, be prepared for the worst, and plan for the best in any number of potentially bad scenarios.

Make a long list of "what if" questions regarding possible equipment failures and potential disasters for your productivity. Consider what resources you have currently or would need to have available as back-up options for your critical equipment and functions. Prioritize the list of additional options, alternatives, resources or tangible pieces of equipment you need to have available.

And don't forget the Murphy's Laws applicable here:

❢ If anything can go wrong, it will.

❢ If multiple things can go wrong simultaneously, they will.

TRANSFER IT PROMPTLY TO IMPROVE PERFORMANCE

 ## Be Prepared With the Basic Tools, Too

Even if you pride yourself on having the most wired, leading edge, technologically advanced home office, you know there are a plethora of low-tech, unexciting, but vital things you just need to have to telecommute and survive. We're not talking about the latest gadgets technology companies are dreaming up to simplify the lives of telecommuters (like scanners that work in the shower, fax machines that also fold your laundry, videophones that will attend meetings for you, and voice-activated software that gives you feedback on your ideas and will write all your reports and memos for you). No, these tools and supplies are much more mundane that this! But don't think about trying to telecommute without equipping yourself with these basics:

• The perfect desk (Tip 88)
• The perfect chair (Tip 93)

- A great phone and phone accessories (Tip 89, Tip 92)
- Rolodex
- Fax, copier, scanner, etc. (Tip 88)
- Extra toner
- Bookcases
- File cabinets
- Power strips, with surge protection (Tip 86)
- File folders and labels
- Storage cabinet (or an alternative)
- Carpeting that's suitable for office use and wear (and is static-free)
- Chair/floor mats to protect carpeting and keep you on the move
- Lamps, task lighting, ambient lighting
- Trash cans —close to your desk, the copier, the printer, wherever you prepare the mail (don't forget to separate recyclables)
- Spare batteries
- Staplers—standard ones wherever you might need one handy, along with specialty types you might need, such as electric, heavy-duty, long-neck (don't forget the staples and stapler removers)
- Rulers, yard stick, tape measurer
- Tape—transparent, double-sided, shipping, masking, correcting, and the ever-important, will-fix-anything roll of duct tape—tape dispensers
- Hole punches—standard for 3-ring binders, adjustable as required, 5- or 7-hole punch if you use a paper-based calendar binder
- Binders and folders
- Pens, pencils, water-based markers, hi-liters—in a variety of colors, sizes, points; for a wide variety of needs/preferences, along with refills and erasers
- Scissors—located in all the places you might need them: your desk, near the copier if you cut and paste, etc.

- Clocks
- Paper cutter
- Disk and CD holders
- Variety of rubber bands, paper clips, binder clips, push pins/tacks and other assorted clips/fasteners in various sizes to hold things together
- Paper towels/tissues
- Supply of various papers, such as copier, laser, bond, card stock, notepads, lined, unlined, drilled for binder use, multiple colors
- Calculator
- Self-stick notes in various sizes (how did we function before these were invented?!) and an assortment of self-stick 'flags' for a multitude of purposes
- Labels—in a variety of sizes, shapes, and colors for shipping, file folders, report or proposal covers, etc.
- Letter opener and utility knife
- Easel, flip chart, corkboard wall, dry erase board or large bulletin board—making ideas visible
- Rubber stamps—for date stamping received mail, quickly handling bank deposits, return addressing; use self-inking when possible
- Postage scale or meter and stamps in various denominations
- Electric pencil sharpener
- Flash light
- Calendars—posted in various locations and viewable from every work station
- Desk accessories to keep everything handy (within arm's reach and to minimize the need to open drawers

For your personal needs, it's convenient to keep these basic things handy:
- Manicure set (or clippers and a nail file)
- Tooth brush and tooth paste

- First aid kit (plastic bandages, at least)
- CD/tape player
- Hand lotion
- Water-free, sanitizing hand cleanser
- Cleaning supplies for eye glasses or contact lenses
- Stress-relief toys, e.g., something to squeeze or fidget with
- Pitcher or large bottle of water
- Small supply of your favorite healthy snack
- Coffee pot and supplies
- Small refrigerator (if it saves you trips to the kitchen and does not become the keeper of things that are bad for you!)

You're likely to identify a few additional MUST HAVE basics for your office (or eliminate some on the list above), depending upon your business, your working style, your office design, and your personal needs/preferences. Since successful telecommuting requires more thoughtful planning and preparation than simply buying a desk, a chair, and a computer, you'll be more productive sooner if you anticipate your needs and carefully prepare your office so that it's "ready to go" when you are.

TIP²

If you're just preparing to telecommute, make a thorough list of the resources, tools, and supplies you'll need. While being prepared is smart, don't overdo it; equip yourself with things you'll need on a regular basis. For resources you'll need only occasionally, consider options like rental, lease, or subcontract. Also, don't overstock supplies that may have a limited shelf life (toner-based products, ink pens).

If you're already telecommuting, make a list of resources you don't have readily available that you need on a regular basis, things you run low on, things you make special trips out of your office to get. Replenish and expand your supplies, tools, and resources to improve your productivity.

TRANSFER IT PROMPTLY TO IMPROVE PERFORMANCE

86 Get Wired—Electrify Your Telecommuting Experience

Inherent in the well-connected, high-tech office of the modern telecommuter is a fundamental reality: wires, cords, and all things electrical. The degree to which you require adequate electrical service cannot be overemphasized from both a capacity and a safety perspective. Without anticipating your electrical needs, it's likely your demand for outlets, extension cords, and power strips will soon overwhelm the electrical system in your house (or at least the circuits supporting your office area). This is a particular concern for older homes and any dwellings not designed for extreme electrical usage in a concentrated area.

Having been one of those telecommuters who added the additional circuits and outlets *after* demand had far exceeded the original outlet capacity in my office, I speak with experience (and eternal gratefulness for the fire I miraculously avoided in my office!). Even I was amazed, however, when I thought to count the number of cords and wires behind my desk. Bear in mind that 4 additional computers, 2 printers, 1 Zip drive, 1 CD-rom drive, 1 transcription machine, 4 lamps, 1 typewriter, 1 electric pencil sharpener, and 1 cassette/tape player are also located in the office but are not on or near the wires behind my desk. Even so, I was stunned to count 39 separate cords and wires flowing off and behind my desk! No, I don't do video production and editing with a massive wall of audio, video, and engineering equipment. These 39 wires support my basic computer system, fax machine, multiple phone lines, videoconference computer, and lighting.

So, keep in mind (I'm living proof, apparently!), those wires can add up and, though it may seem so, they're not multiplying while you sleep. To keep yourself, your office, and your equipment safe, keep some key guidelines in mind so that your wired office doesn't exceed the capacity of your electrical system.

- Unless you're an electrical engineer or a certified electrician, remember that being a highly-skilled home handyperson does not qualify you to run wire, add outlets, and expand the number of circuits feeding your office. This is definitely a time to spend a few dollars, protect the safety of your family and your office, and avoid problems with insurance claims filed in connection with work performed during your "temporary electrician" stint! Electricity is great, but it's nothing to mess around with unless you really know what you're doing.

- Avoid extension cords wherever possible. If you must use them, use high-grade extension cords or power strips.

- In spite of having plenty of outlets, you'll probably still need some power strips. Use only those designed for use with sensitive electronic equipment (like your computer) that provide maximum protection against power surges. Be aware that power surge protection may not be effective against electrical surges that enter your home through phone lines connected to your equipment. Therefore, for maximum protection, use high-end surge protectors that include connected equipment warranties.

- And don't forget to UNPLUG (not just turn off) your equipment during a storm and avoid using the telephone during electrical storms.

TIP²

! If you have any doubt about the excessive demand your equipment may be making on your electrical system, pick up the phone right now and schedule a visit by the electrician.

! In the meantime, be sure that all of your critical equipment has appropriate power surge protection.

! And to avoid confusion at critical moments, be sure you know which breakers or fuses support which electrical lines. These should be clearly marked in your breaker or fuse box.

Computer Choices and Conundrums

When you telecommute, your computer is typically a tool that's vital to your ability to accomplish work. Unless your employer provides a standard-issue machine with supporting hardware (this can certainly simplify your life!), you'll need to determine the best equipment for your individual situation. Once again, begin with determining your needs:

- What are the primary purposes for your computer?

- What software applications will you require?

- Therefore, what will you require in terms of speed, memory, and storage capacity? (Never underestimate here; buying more capacity initially is usually the best course of action.)

- Which operating system is most appropriate (or required) to communicate with co-workers?

- What demands will you be making on the modem for high-speed transmission of data?

- What type of keyboard, monitor, mouse, and Zip drive will you need to support your primary applications and future needs?

- Will you travel frequently? Would a notebook computer and docking station or port replicator be a better alternative for you?

- What needs do you have for a primary (and secondary) printer?

- How likely is it that you'll need to upgrade the equipment or expand its capacity?

- Do you have the required electrical capacity in your office? (Tip 86)

- Do you have an appropriate work station in your office (a computer table or desk with space for the monitor and keyboard at appropriate heights and the printer within easy reach)?

- What level of technical support will you require for installation and ongoing needs?

Once you've formulated your specifications based on your needs, review them with:

- The computer support team that best knows the systems and applications used by your company. Ask for input, recommendations, directives, or constraints you should know about. Also confirm the level of support they will be able to provide you.

- A knowledgeable sales associate at a major computer retail outlet.

- A computer consultant, whom you also may secure to do the legwork involved in evaluating equipment options, reviewing current price offerings (in stores, from catalog distributors, on the Internet), and making a purchase recommendation to you.

Don't hesitate to get the help you need in sorting through the maze of options, features, bells, and whistles. At a minimum, unless you're very savvy with regard to computer technology and equipment, find someone (or hire someone as part of your equipment purchase) to handle the setup and installation of your new system and to train you on the basics. When I bought a new computer and printer several years ago, I got the help of a high-tech young man who thought that spending a day buying and installing my whole system was the highlight of his spring break. (And, of course, the "ready to go/just pop it out of the box" promise from the manufacturer did not materialize into reality, so I was able to be very productive doing other things while my young consultant spent hours on the phone with technical support folks.) Again, unless it's a hobby for you or you are extremely challenged by such things, get some help with installation, setup, and any time-consuming loading or transferring of software and files. If you're really a focused telecommuter, you should have lots of other higher priority ways to invest your time and energy.

TIP²

🖳 If you're in the market for a new computer and/or peripheral equipment, use the process described above to define your needs and explore the best match in terms of equipment and services.

🖳 If you already have your computer system in place, consider any enhancements or peripherals you need to improve your productivity or your use of the computer's capabilities. Define your needs (Tip 83) for any additional hardware, software, or services that might benefit you and "shop your specs" in the most appropriate and time-efficient way for you (hire a consultant, search the Web, peruse catalogs, do one-stop shopping at your favorite computer superstore, etc.).

TRANSFER IT PROMPTLY TO IMPROVE PERFORMANCE

 Beyond the Computer: Essential Tools (and Toys) for the Well-Connected Telecommuter

One of the long-standing myths about telecommuting is that it's so simple to do; just stay home, flip open a wireless notebook computer, grab your cell phone, and hang out at the pool. Let me be clear (did I harp on this once before?!): Nothing could be further from the truth about serious telecommuting. Of course I've taken my cell phone to the pool, but usually it's because I'm still working when everyone else is playing! Telecommuting effectively requires concentrated effort, dedicated time, and all the right tools.

Since you usually won't be working poolside, having a great **desk** is an excellent idea. As with other equipment you'll need, first determine your needs and preferences.

☞ How do you plan to use your desk?

☞ Will your computer be located on or in it? What type of work will you be doing at your desk?

☞ Will you need to have a wide expanse of flat work surface? Or will you require easy access to drawers full of files?

☞ Would you prefer a stand-up work surface rather than a traditional desk?

☞ How much space do you have available for the desk of your dreams?

Take your needs and preferences to an office furniture store and start-field testing different desks and desk arrangements. Be sure to check into modular designs, as well as traditional desks. As with other major purchases, be sure you can return the desk if it proves to be the wrong choice.

Aside from your desk, you'll probably need a **fax** machine, unless you plan to let your computer function as the fax machine. Of course, you'll need to have a dedicated line and computer that stays on all the time, which is a problem if it's the notebook computer you take on the road. Other considerations in determining your needs for a fax:

- While other technology still is marketed, plain paper machines (with plenty of capacity in the paper tray) is by far the easiest option.

- Multi-purpose fax machines are useful if your copying, printing and scanning needs are not excessive or you have other equipment for these purposes and the multi-purpose fax provides your back-up options (Tip 84).

- Look for other valuable features like delayed transmission (fax while you sleep!), speed dial, automatic redial, activity reports, memory capacity, resolution, transmission speed, image size adjustment, integration with your computer, service warranties, and ongoing maintenance and ink replacement requirements.

You may or may not have copying needs that justify having a **copier** in your office. In many cases, a multi-purpose fax will suffice. Or using the services of a local quick-print will be more than adequate. However, if external copying sources are not convenient and/or your copying needs exceed more than a handful of copies per day, an on-site machine that you buy or lease may be best for you. Consider your needs and evaluate features such as:

- Projected copy volume
- Ease of operation
- Speed
- Paper requirements
- Paper tray capacity
- Image size adjustment
- Types of documents copied (e.g., size of paper, books, magazine articles, etc.), color versus black-and-white

▤ Routine maintenance, table or stand required, storage of supplies, toner replacement, and ongoing service/technical support.

Since everyone's definition of "essential" will vary somewhat, there
isn't one standard list of required equipment for telecommuters.
Depending on your needs, your office arrangement, your line of
work, and your personal work habits, there are any number of other
items that may be either essential tools or gotta-have-'em toys for
you:

- Personal pager
- Notebook computer
- Personal digital assistant
- Microcassette recorder
- Personal dictating/transcription machines
- Paper shredder
- Postage meter
- Adapters for your computer (to use with car cigarette lighter
  and cellular phone)

Depending on your need to travel as part of your telecommuting
agreement, your list of mandatory "road warrior" tools may get
longer. If you do travel more than occasionally, don't forget the utterly low-tech but very important briefcase or backpack or rolling
luggage in which to transport all of your high-tech gizmos.

And finally, cool as all the gizmology may be, avoid gadgets that
are unnecessary, don't interface well with your primary equipment,
are not proven in terms of effectiveness and reliability, take more
time to use than they save, and do little more than appeal to your
bias for "gee-whiz-bang" gadgetry.

TIP²

- ⌨ What additional technology resources might help you be more
  effective and productive?
- ⌨ What tools (or toys) do you have currently that are not proving
  to be very useful?

📠 Reevaluate your needs for additional tools that can help you be a more successful telecommuter and take steps to match those needs with appropriate and cost-effective choices.

TRANSFER IT PROMPTLY TO IMPROVE PERFORMANCE

 ## Rarely Is a Phone Just a Phone

With so much of your telecommuting technology dependent upon telephone lines, what you need and require from your phone service provider(s) differs significantly from your needs in the not-too-distant past. Likewise, what you need in terms of capabilities in your actual phone equipment has changed dramatically. Not too long ago, a phone with 10 speed dial numbers and a hold button was fairly sophisticated. Now a telecommuter would compare the benefits of integral phone systems versus Web phones versus wireless technology.

Depending upon your needs, your budget, the level of technology sophistication of your employer, and the capacity of the phone wiring in your home, you may have the opportunity to utilize some of these advanced technologies. In the meantime, though, the cautiously or budget-constrained innovators who also telecommute probably will still use telephones. Thankfully, your telephone can be far more advanced than a basic phone and make important contributions to your productivity. Evaluate your requirements for telephonic technology by considering your need for features such as:

☎ *Multiple lines.* You're likely to have multiple phone lines coming into your home to support voice, fax, and data transmissions. Don't limit your ability to access all of these lines when you need them for additional voice calls or conference calling by using phones that don't support multiple lines. You can easily accommodate up to four lines on an individual phone without the expense of an advanced telephone system. Using more than one 4-line phone allows you to establish a basic office system with features such as intercom/paging, transferring, do not disturb, and monitoring. If you're trying to integrate business and home lines, this can be a big help.

☎ *Voice mail.* Some phones come equipped with advanced voice mail systems that save you the expense of monthly voice mail charges from your phone company. With some of these you can also establish individual voice mail boxes, so these systems offer a very professional image.

☎ *Caller ID.* This feature might be of interest to you if want to prioritize specific callers or avoid interrupting a call in progress for a nonessential incoming call.

☎ *Speed dialing/memory dial.* For frequently dialed numbers, this can be a critical time saver. Some telephones also will integrate with auto-dialing capability through your computer. Even without the computer connection, however, make sure the primary phone that sits closest to your work area has a generous capacity for numbers in memory.

☎ *Automatic redial.* Like speed dialing, this is a convenient and time-saving feature. It's especially useful for numbers you don't have programmed into memory. When you dial the number and get a busy signal, your phone will continue to periodically dial the number (for a set number of attempts or a specific length of time) until the call is answered—all the while, you're busy doing other productive things.

☎ *Speakerphone.* While some people just despise being relegated to your speakerphone, this feature can be very helpful to you for hands-free telephone time (especially during long conference calls). On the flip side, however, a speakerphone in a one-room office in your home (or anywhere for that matter) would be very annoying if others also were working there. Some of the advantages of having a speakerphone can be achieved by using a headset (Tip 92).

☎ *Call waiting.* If you use multiple voice lines for business, this feature may be unnecessary. And some people find it very annoying or distracting. However, it may be convenient to have on days you're expecting an important call. On other days, you can ignore the call waiting signal and let the call roll over to voice mail if you're already involved in a call you don't want to interrupt.

☎ *Conferencing*. Many basic business phones come equipped with three-way calling for establishing conference calls. You may find the audio quality lacking on some phones when the third caller is added. If conferencing is a critical feature for you, test this feature thoroughly on your new phone, establish conference-calling capability through your phone company, or schedule conference calls through your long distance carrier (also a more viable option if you need to connect multiple people and locations).

☎ *Call forwarding*. This is usually a feature available through your phone company and can be an important one for telecommuters who are committed to staying well connected to co-workers, clients, and colleagues (Tip 52). If you need to leave your office for errands, a meeting, a networking lunch, or travel, you can forward your phone to wherever you go.

☎ *Mute*. This comes in handy during long conference calls or when your spouse stops in with a quick question. And it certainly is a handy feature if you have an unexpected visit from a well-intended but somewhat loud child!

☎ *Call timer*. If you need to track your calls for billing purposes, you'll appreciate this feature. Otherwise, it's also useful to keep yourself aware of the length of calls.

☎ *Number dialed and time display*. On really hectic days, this feature is nice in case you forget who you were calling in the space of time between dialing the call and hearing it ring! Also, since your phone is probably fairly convenient, this gives you a quick look at the time of day.

☎ *Volume control*. Depending on your voice, the connection quality with your caller, and the effect that a headset may have on the audio level on your phone line, volume control is a useful feature for achieving the best connection possible within the constraints of your equipment and the quality of the line provided by your carrier.

☎ *Cordless*. Adding a cordless phone to one of your extensions gives you flexibility to move around for accessing files, information, or other computers in your office. During long (or less exciting) calls, you also can roam to the kitchen for a quick snack or to the back yard to enjoy your flower garden.

Other accessories you might find useful:

☎ *Answering machine.* If you don't have voice mail or want to screen calls, a separate answering machine might be the best choice for you.

☎ *Cord detangler.* An absolute must if tangled cords make you crazy. (When they get really out of control, save yourself the frustration and buy a new cord.)

☎ *Extra long cord.* If you don't have a headset or cordless phone but want to roam, this will surely help.

☎ *Video phone.* Really fun—if you need it, of course, and if you call other people who have one.

Your phone can do even more to help you be productive if your local phone company offers additional capabilities you need. Since your phone is so integral to your work as a telecommuter, don't hesitate to let it work for you to get the most it can give.

TIP²

ℂ Check your existing phone capabilities against a list of ideal features to maximize your productivity.

ℂ Prepare a spec sheet to evaluate the cost versus the benefits of investing in a new phone.

ℂ Check to be certain there aren't any features on your existing phone that you haven't activated or don't use.

TRANSFER IT PROMPTLY TO IMPROVE PERFORMANCE

Make Your Phone Calls Chase or Wait for You

In your quest to stay well connected while telecommuting, you're likely to find numerous ways to get information to and from people with great efficiency. Also, you're likely to find that you feel bombarded by the influx of voice messages, calls, faxes, and e-mail messages. In reality, however, the volume of calls and demand for your attention is probably no greater than what you'd experience working in a traditional office. Only the nature of some interruptions differ in that people usually can't just "drop in" on you. (Beware, however, if your employer launches a videoconferencing system and you keep your system turned on constantly. Based on my experience, people will begin "dropping by" virtually. This is especially intrusive if you set your videoconference or videophone system on "auto answer." You may hear a phone ring and suddenly find people staring at you!)

Of course, you'll often *want* to be accessible to people—regardless of where you are—and to be almost as available as if you were physically present in the main office or at the client site. And at other times you'll need to defer your calls to voice mail or some other answering system. Whichever option is appropriate for a given situation or time, be certain to handle it in the most suitable way for capturing the information people need to give you.

When you want to be connected and highly accessible by phone, having multiple business lines for voice transmission is useful. Otherwise, your calls will be greeted with either call waiting, an answering machine, answering service, or voice mail (or, God forbid, a busy signal!). So, look for ways to increase the opportunity to answer a call "live," even though you might need to return the call if it will take longer than you have available. If you do need to defer your calls to one of your answering systems due to a client meeting, conference call, personal appointment, or during nonwork hours, be sure to:

- ℂ Be as specific as possible about when you'll be available or when you'll be able to return the call.
- ℂ Check for messages frequently.
- ℂ Return calls promptly.

When you are out of the office but don't want to miss any calls, activate your call forwarding feature. (With the advent of new rate plans for cellular calling that provides hundreds of minutes per month of calling time without roaming or long distance charges, there may be an increase in telecommuters using cellular phones as their primary business phone. Also, the future promises the eventual opportunity for you to have one number that rings everywhere—in your office, in your home, on your cellular phone wherever you are, etc.) Calls can easily be forwarded to your cell phone and, with a reliable cellular provider, your calls will follow you just about anywhere.

If for some reason your cellular service is unavailable, another option is to forward your calls to the voice mail on your personal pager. If you need to receive calls at home, forward your business line to your home phone. (For a nominal charge, your phone company might offer an identifying ring capability for your home line to differentiate business calls from personal calls.) You also can forward your business line to other office locations where you'll be working for the day or week. This might be at your corporate office or a client site. Clearly, being "out of sight" when you telecommute never needs to mean being "out of touch."

 TIP²

Review the way your calls are handled when you're away from your office.

☎ Is your current answering or voice mail system the best available option? Are you receiving prompt, clear, and thorough messages? Are you retrieving messages in a timely fashion and responding quickly enough?

☎ Do you need to be more accessible when you're out of the office? Are you experiencing delays in receiving critical information, frustration from co-workers, or dissatisfaction from clients? What alternatives can you employ or acquire to improve your access to timely information and your accessibility to people who need to contact you?

TRANSFER IT PROMPTLY TO IMPROVE PERFORMANCE

 ## Manage the Madness of Multiple Machines that Ring or Beep at You

Once you're functioning as a well-connected telecommuter with multiple ways for people to contact you and for the exchange of information, you also may begin to feel a sense of intrusion. Depending upon the degree of connectivity you have with the "world" beyond your office, there can be a wide assortment of equipment interrupting the serenity of your telecommuting space and demanding your immediate attention:

- ♨ Multiple phone lines ringing and flashing.
- ♨ Voice mail signals and greetings announcing the accumulation of an astronomical number of messages in your voice mail box.
- ♨ Flashes and incessant beeps from the answering machine.
- ♨ The pager that beeps or vibrates with demands that you call your answering service for messages.
- ♨ E-mail messages that land in your in-box with a loud "kerplunk" sound (programmed into your computer by some well-intentioned but humorless computer technician).
- ♨ The cellular phone that rings (with a unique ring you selected from an almost endless array of options), flashes, or vibrates to announce the arrival of a call, a page, or even an e-mail message.

How do you manage it all without pulling out your hair (and/or all those wires)!? First of all, simplify. If you have one of those wonderful new cell phones that will deliver voice calls, data, e-mail messages, and pages, perhaps it's time to discontinue using your personal pager. Keep the pager if you really need to receive pages during flights, if your cellular service is unreliable in some areas where you work, or if you're occasionally on-call for some extremely urgent purpose (such as performing emergency brain surgery). Also, unless you're using your cellular phone as your primary business line, think twice about keeping your cell phone on when you're in the office (unless it's a "hot-line" for access to you by critical clients or you really enjoy juggling yet another ringing phone during the workday).

Finally, be selective about when you accept incoming calls and messages. Voice mail and e-mail messages may drop into your in-box constantly, but if you respond to them as they arrive, you'll compromise your ability to manage your work in a planful and proactive way. Set aside specific time throughout the day to read faxes and e-mail messages and to listen to voice mail messages. Do this frequently and respond to them promptly, with as much brevity as possible. Without planning and exercising control over how you respond to everything that rings or beeps, you'll be relegated to days of incessant interruptions demanding reactive and frantic responses. This will not only exhaust and frustrate you, it will also compromise your success as a telecommuter and undermine your attainment of the personal and business goals you chose to pursue as a telecommuter.

And it should go without needing a mention (except that another reminder probably won't hurt), it remains your responsibility to either shut everything off or close the door to your office or ignore anything in your office that rings or beeps when it's time to set work aside. The eternal quest for balance (Tip 6) gets no easier as the technology to access you improves. Only now, you need to manage both your need for balance and the technology that can threaten it.

 TIP²

➡ Review the various ways your work flow is interrupted by calls, messages, and other electronic demands for your attention.

➡ Can you streamline the number of incoming sources of beeps and rings?

➡ Reevaluate how and when you respond and look for increased ways to protect your focus.

TRANSFER IT PROMPTLY TO IMPROVE PERFORMANCE

92 Skip the Massage— Get a Headset

Unless you telecommute with minimal need to interact by telephone with co-workers, customers, or associates, having a headset is something you should seriously consider. I know no one who's tried using a headset and decided to go back to the neck-killing phone on the shoulder routine. At the same time, I know any number of people who've been disappointed with a headset they purchased for one reason or another. If your phone usage justifies it, a headset is an invaluable tool for a telecommuter, but there's great variability among headsets in terms of comfort, audio quality, and operating flexibility. So, put a headset on your list of essential tools and evaluate these features when selecting one:

- Weight (the lighter the better)
- Adjustability (to accommodate your unique configuration and combination of personal features: head, ear, hair, glasses, earrings)
- Range (depending upon your need to access files and reference material or your need to pace)
- Volume control (to accommodate variations in voice level of callers and clarity of phone lines)
- Microphone (get the best you can afford so you don't sound as if you're calling from Mars)
- Wireless (provides the greatest mobility, with compromises in sound quality unless you're willing to not go cheap)
- Service, warranty, and maintenance (ask for comparisons of durability and typical projected useful life of various models).

As with other key tools and equipment for your telecommuting success, purchase a headset only if you have the option to return it. Since it spends long hours hanging on your ear or strapped to your head, you want to absolutely love it and be extremely comfortable with it as an appendage. It's rather like a pair of shoes: If it doesn't feel great, you won't use it. If you can't return it for a more suitable one, you've wasted your money. Even worse, you'll have that phone locked between your ear and your spasm-riddled neck.

TIP^2

- ✆ If you're currently using a headset, check out newer models and consider whether upgrading would improve your comfort and productivity.
- ✆ If you're still using a hand-held telephone, spending lots of time on it, and suffering from neck and shoulder pain, add "GET A HEADSET" to the top of your TO DO list. Check options available through your local office superstore, catalog companies

that specialize in these products (such as Hello Direct!), and Internet sources. Order more than one type or model to give yourself a choice of features and the greatest degree of comfort.

 ## Which Chair to Buy (When You'd Really Rather Have a Recliner)

The closest thing to you (literally) when you telecommute is your chair. Since you might sometimes feel that you live in your office chair (and in a way, you do), invest in a superb one; you'll never regret it. In spite of an abundance of seldom-used chairs sprinkled throughout your home, don't be tempted to opt for convenience by grabbing one of these. And certainly don't target aesthetics among your primary criteria. How your chair looks in your office and integrates with your design scheme is fairly insignificant (unless winning decorating awards is a key objective) compared with the other features you should evaluate when buying a desk chair:

- *Well-constructed and provides excellent support.* Look for high-quality materials, solid but comfortable support in the seat and back, and a fabric that won't cause you to perspire (there are enough other things to sweat over!) or slide off the chair as you roll from one task to another.

- *Ergonomically designed for your body.* Not all chairs fit all body types, so ask questions, read the manufacturer's specs, road-test different styles, and, if you still can't find the perfect chair, have one custom-built (it will probably be the last desk chair you'll ever need to buy, so the investment will be worth it).

- *Provides adjustability, flexibility, and mobility.* At a minimum, you need to adjust the seat height, back tilt, and lumbar support to accommodate the different tasks you'll undertake in a given day. Aim for flexibility that allows you to swivel, tilt, recline, and rock, while riding on a five-star base with self-locking, dual casters. Consider the type of flooring your chair will rest on in determining the specific type of caster you need.

- *Offers you a high degree of comfort.* The chair makes your body feel supported, relaxed, and ready to work. Consider a chair with armrests if they add to your comfort, support your arms at the appropriate heights, and don't interfere with your desk or computer work station.

- *Option to purchase on a trial basis.* Be sure to learn the proper way to sit in the chair, and adjust it to your body and the tasks you perform in your office. Use it in your office for several typical work days before making a final decision to purchase. Return it in a flash if it doesn't fit you or your desk in a comfortable and productive way.

A top-quality desk chair will not be inexpensive. On the other hand, it's a great investment compared to the time and money you'll end up spending with a chiropractor if you shortchange yourself on the quality you deserve (and need) in a first-rate chair. Don't overlook your need for additional chairs, as well. An experienced telecommuter I know thought this was the best tip in this book! He's a big advocate of having an excellent chair, but also of having a different one for different activities. Therefore, he has, in addition to his desk chair, a task chair for use when he's working at his computer, and a reading chair (not a recliner!), since his work involves heavy doses of reading. If your office is large enough, consider investing in additional chairs for multiple needs.

And finally, even if it's a great chair and you spent a small fortune on it, your body (and your mind) will still benefit from periodic respites from a sitting position. Intersperse all that productivity you're achieving as a result of using a fabulous chair with standing, walking, and stretching for at least 30 seconds every 30 minutes.

 TIP²

Visit an office furniture store sometime soon to evaluate the choices in quality desk chairs. Carefully select one that meets your needs and is suited for your body and office. If you already have a desk chair, compare yours against those that may offer far greater comfort and productivity.

TRANSFER IT PROMPTLY TO IMPROVE PERFORMANCE

94 Learn to Love Voice Mail (and Other Impossibilities)

Voice mail is a much-maligned technological advance. It's a bit like the annoyance we feel about having to *empty* the dishwasher, completely overlooking the utter convenience and time savings we derive from not needing to hand-wash all those dishes! Voice mail suffers a similar lack of respect and appreciation. However, the flexibility and productivity you gain from voice messaging enables, in part, your ability to telecommute, so I wouldn't be too annoyed about its existence.

Without voice mail you would spend far more time in the completely unproductive game of telephone tag. True, now you play voice mail tag. But, used effectively, voice mail can drastically minimize the level of "tag time" and the number of interruptions in your day. Additionally, voice mail is a critical communication vehicle for people who work remotely, are in "road warrior" mode, are in widely distant locales around the globe, or have limited time between meetings to exchange information.

Voice mail is the first widely used and now commonly accepted technology that helped pave the way for telecommuting. It established initial experience (and growing comfort) with virtual interactions. Some people have even come to prefer voice mail for its efficiency and its complete flexibility to be used anytime of the day (or night). For example, I once worked with a woman who was implementing a client project for my sales team and with whom I needed to exchange up-to-the-minute information regarding the project. Even though she generally called it a day and was asleep by 9:30 PM (when my "second wind" was just picking up), we successfully completed our work together thanks to voice mail. I typically left project update messages by 2:30 AM, which she retrieved and responded to when she woke up around 4:30 AM; I picked up her messages when I awoke (at a more civilized hour). Voice mail provided the medium by which we communicated with relative speed and effectiveness. More people now realize that voice mail can facilitate a great deal of communication that would otherwise be very difficult.

E-mail has replaced some uses of voice mail since it offers the advantage of being more tangible (at least you can *see* it!) and can be saved or printed for future reference. Also, when documents must be exchanged or messages are lengthy, e-mail is certainly superior. Otherwise, voice mail is clearly advantageous for messages that are:

- *Brief* ("I'm working on a prospective sale and would appreciate your input on a few issues. When are you available to meet tomorrow?")

- *Time-urgent* ("I'm running 20 minutes late for our lunch meeting, but I'll meet you there.")

- *Appropriate to the technology* (Don't leave messages regarding sensitive, confidential, or performance-related issues. Rather, leave a voice message requesting a voice-to-voice or face-to-face conversation for such matters.)

Voice mail is particularly effective if there's a bias throughout the entire organization for checking messages frequently and responding with promptness, completeness, and brevity. Leaving a time-urgent message is safer if you can count on the recipient to check messages often. (Otherwise, have the person paged or leave a message with a "live" human who agrees to relay the message quickly.) When voice mail is seen not as one more thing to get through during the day (or late at night), rather than one more way to improve our efficiency and timeliness in communicating with co-workers, clients, and colleagues, its value is diminished and its utility greatly compromised. It's a valuable telecommuting tool, and one you should employ frequently and skillfully.

 TIP²

Review your voice mail greeting to confirm that it provides thorough information about when you will:

✆ Check messages

✆ Return calls

✆ Be available to talk with the caller

Also, verify that your greeting requests thorough messages from your callers: name, time/day of the call, information or action requested of you and by when, voice mail or phone number you'll need for responding to the message.

TRANSFER IT PROMPTLY TO IMPROVE PERFORMANCE

95 Videoconferencing: The Next Best Thing to Being There?

Yes, videoconferencing probably *is* the next best thing to being there, but that doesn't mean it's as effective or can be used without some serious planning (and a not-so-minor investment). While the promise of picturephones has never quite been fulfilled at a reasonable cost, videoconferencing is an emerging technology application that will further revolutionize and strengthen the telecommuting trend. It's probably also the tool that generates the highest degree of discomfort, primarily because of weaknesses inherent in affordable systems that exacerbate the anxieties people feel about using the technology.

Many people, if they're honest, aren't really comfortable in front of a regular old camera that shoots prints. Imagine the anxiety these folks have in the presence of a video camera that captures their every move, doesn't necessarily offer them an image of how they appear to other participants, and transmits their image to multiple sites in distant locations. Further, anyone the least bit technophobic tends to be rendered practically nonfunctioning at the very thought of speaking into a camera while perhaps needing to simultaneously control screen image, camera projection, audio levels, and a computer. It's not a great formula for accelerated growth in use of the technology, wouldn't you agree? However, as travel costs increase along with peripheral costs associated with face-to-face meetings, the decreases in cost in videoconference equipment and services inevitably will result in more videoconferencing. Telecommuters naturally will be on the forefront of this trend, so anticipate more "on camera" time in your future.

Videoconference systems range from low-end versions using special software and a camera mounted to your computer to more sophisticated, stand-alone systems with a dedicated computer, high-speed modems, and ISDN or T-1 lines. There's also a corresponding range in video quality, audio reception, and, of course, cost. For example, supporting a videoconference system with a slow modem or single ISDN line will produce choppy video with obvious audio delays. This can be so distracting and uncomfortable to some people that videoconferencing loses its appeal and is seen as inferior to audio-only teleconferencing or text-based Web conferencing.

While the notion of real-time videoconferencing as an integral part of telecommuting has great appeal, it is viable only if transmission speed is appropriate. Additionally, equipment and software compatibility is critical. Videoconferencing is essentially an application of computer technology, and you know how badly things work when incompatible software or hardware is being used. While there are some standard videoconferencing protocols, there is not a commonly used standard throughout the industry that ensures your ability to establish a videoconference link with just anyone (as you can do almost universally with fax technology, in spite of great variation in equipment and manufacturers).

If you will be using videoconference technology in spite of its limitations, it offers many advantages over audio-only connections. Provided the video quality is good, you can observe gestures, facial expressions, and body language, all of which can enhance communication and strengthen distance relationships. To achieve this, however, you'll need to be clear about how and with whom you'll use videoconferencing; and be careful to use a technology platform that's consistent with the equipment and software located at the sites you'll be connecting to. Once you have the appropriate software, hardware, and transmission vehicle (e.g., ISDN, Internet) in place, be sure to prepare people to effectively use this tool (Tip 65). Videoconferencing promises to play an important and growing role in the life of a telecommuter, so stay tuned!

TIP²

🖥 If you're currently using a videoconference system, consider ways you can improve your use of the system and the effectiveness of the videoconferences in which you participate. Talk to your manager and the appropriate technology resource for your company to explore equipment enhancements that will improve the caliber of the videoconference system.

🖥 If your employer currently is not using videoconferences as a way to connect telecommuters to other team members, initiate a task force to investigate alternative systems, costs, and benefits.

96 Meet the Challenge of Internet Connections

On some days, zooming along the Internet is more fiction than fact. You may simply chug along because of:

- An antiquated modem that's nowhere near ready to wear out, but it's still woefully outdated.

- Some kind of problem (that resembles something like a personality clash) between your software and your computer.

- Access problems of unknown origin—you know only that the phone company is sure that your Internet Service Provider (ISP) is the cause and your ISP is certain it's a problem at the phone company.

Either way, you're stuck and going nowhere fast. This is an unacceptable and exasperating situation for a telecommuter, since so much of your connection to the world beyond your home office is likely to depend on speedy navigation of the Internet. If you access your corporate e-mail, network, and Internet via the Web, you must have the equipment, software, and services necessary to achieve speed and reliability for your Internet connections. You also may rely on the Internet for accessing resource information, news retrieval services, bulletin boards, newsgroups, listserves, personal e-mail, and a wide range of professional and industry sites and contacts that are critical to your networking efforts. Therefore, reliable access to the Internet is vital to your success (and ability to minimize stress) when you telecommute.

If you're experiencing problems with your equipment and don't know (or want to know) the intricacies of modem performance specs, consult your computer consultant, your corporate network team or help-desk, or a knowledgeable resource in your network to get the help you need. If you're caught between your phone company and your ISP, don't count on them to work it out. When faced with similar problems, I've arranged and mediated conference calls on several occasions between technicians at my phone company and technicians with other providers that access my phone lines. I didn't always understand everything (or, sometimes, much!) of what they were discussing, but I made sure they talked voice-to-voice, I made sure everyone understood how the problem was being experienced, and I didn't let anyone hang up until we reached "Eureka!" and found a solution.

Unless you specialize in Internet access or happen to be an expert in Web technology, the range of alternatives available for accessing the Internet will make your head spin: broadband, asymmetrical digital subscriber line (ADSL), integrated services digital network (ISDN), cable modems, and anything else introduced between the writing and reading of this information. The availability, cost, and service offerings of ISPs varies widely. Therefore, you need to research what's available in your area, compare services against your needs, evaluate initial and ongoing costs against your budget, and choose the option that provides the best solution for you. If you are not accessing the Internet through an ISP contracted by your employer, reference the following criteria when selecting an ISP:

- Local access so you're not incurring toll charges from your phone company.

- Plenty of access lines during peak usage times so you do not encounter busy signals.

- Reasonable cost (based on current prevailing rates) with unlimited access.

- 24-hour (or close to it) technical support provided by real people (no voice mail menus or automated fax services).

If your ISP is not delivering on the service commitments it made, reevaluate your choices and get another one. At the same time, if the limitations of your own system are keeping you off the high-speed lanes, seriously consider upgrading your capabilities and equipment to improve your ability to navigate the Internet with speed and skill.

TIP²

- Look for ways to achieve major or incremental improvements in your access to the Internet.

- Consider how your ISP, your equipment, and your own knowledge and skills might be limiting your effectiveness and efficiency with the Web.

- Take steps to eliminate barriers and implement improvements.

TRANSFER IT PROMPTLY TO IMPROVE PERFORMANCE

97 Have Technology, Will Travel

In the not-too-distant past, when you left your office to travel on business, you pretty much "unplugged" from your normal activities and communication. (You might remember how agonizing it was to "catch up" after some of those extended road trips.) I can recall people referring to themselves being "out of pocket" for the days they'd be gone, and the implication was that regular work would cease, voice-to-voice contact would be minimal at best, and mail would simply pile up in in-baskets until the trip was over. Enter onto the business scene a series of innovations to improve our access to information and connectivity to everyone regardless of where we are: telephone calling cards, lower longer distance rates, telefax technology, and increasing access to readily available public fax machines, voice mail, cellular phones, e-mail, notebook computers that continue shrinking in size and weight, wireless Internet access, personal digital assistants, etc. It's a whole new ball game, and road warriors run the bases between on-line, real-time, and waste-no-time technology solutions that make you feel as if you never really left home after all.

Most telecommuters have opportunities (some occasional, some extremely frequent) to venture forth from their home-based offices to join the ranks of road warriors who definitely are "plugged in" while traveling, though the age of wireless technology is making the reality of plugs in outlets increasingly obsolete. Travel is no longer a reason (or an excuse) to miss a call, delay responses to voice mail, overlook e-mail, or be a "no show" at a regular staff meeting. Of course, this doesn't mean that you won't at times feel as if all this technology is not only intrusive but a burden, as well.

While it's great to have the ability to be so connected, anyone who's done any serious time as a road warrior knows you're often slogging through e-mail messages between a business dinner and your much-needed night's rest to prepare for your 6 A.M. departure on yet another flight to another day of meetings . . . interspersed with voice mail checks while walking to your airline gate . . . conference calls during your lunch break . . . connecting to e-mail during breaks from your meeting . . . so you can read all that e-mail during your flight back home that night and transmit them from the e-mail link the airline conveniently has added to the airphone service . . . allowing you to walk into your office the next morning completely caught up . . . except for the 17 new voice mail messages and 34 new e-mail messages that landed in your electronic in-boxes while you slept!!! If you resonate with this scenario and/or feel a little weary just reading it, you know it's not much of an exaggeration.

Using technology when traveling should help you be more productive, more connected, better informed and, hence, more effective. If you let it overwhelm you or run amok in your attempts to manage it all, you'll be frustrated, tired, and resentful. So here's my advice:

- Carry the minimum amount and lightest weight equipment necessary.

  ⇨ Personal Digital Assistants (PDA) can be a wonderful way to streamline the information and technology essential to your travels. If you don't need the data or capacity of your notebook computer, leave it.

  ⇨ If you haven't yet upgraded to a lightweight (≤ 6 oz.) cellular phone, talk to your cellular provider about how to do so. Get one with a pager included and leave the pager on your desk.

  ⇨ Do you really need that portable printer? Unless you're going someplace where the latest in technology innovation is an electric toothbrush, it's likely you'll find a printer to plug into at your hotel, at the airport business center, or at the local printing/copy center (such as Kinko's).

- Set aside specific times to process new (and critical) voice mail and e-mail messages.

  ⇨ Plan your day (even when your schedule is at the mercy of the airline or train schedule) so you have designated times blocked off for checking messages.

  ⇨ Use any filtering mechanisms your systems offer for prioritizing messages by urgency or by sender.

  ⇨ Delete anything that you don't need to read.

  ⇨ Be brief (and use minimalist courtesy).

- Give yourself a break from it occasionally.

  ⇨ If you're really tired, go to bed. (Your terse and insensitive e-mail will only come back to haunt you.)

⇨ Set a goal to process a targeted number of e-mail messages during your flight. If you hit your target before you're required to stow your electronic equipment, go ahead . . . play a game of solitaire or chess if it helps you relax or keep it all in perspective.

⇨ Allow the intrusion (and expense) of communication by airphone only when it's really necessary. One of the few nice things about being cooped up in an airplane for hours is the relative detachment you have from all the madness on the ground. Whenever you can, give yourself just a bit of serenity for a little while. You might even benefit from time spent cloud gazing!

TIP²

◈ Pull out that well-worn travel bag and reevaluate what you stuff into it when you travel.

◈ Is there a lighter way for you to go?

◈ Consider ways to downsize, eliminate, streamline, and simplify.

◈ At a minimum, evaluate your need for a PDA if you don't have one and think about what you really *need* versus what you automatically just schlep along unnecessarily.

TRANSFER IT PROMPTLY TO IMPROVE PERFORMANCE

 # If Talking to Yourself is Interesting, Try Faxing to Yourself

When you find yourself in a situation where access to a printer is limited or nonexistent, don't forget the fax capability that may be resident in your computer. This is often true when you're in the "road warrior" mode—at a hotel where the business center is closed or the reception desk charges exorbitant rates to print a few pages. If your computer has the necessary software and modem (most machines used by the typical road warrior have this function), simply fax your document (from the comfort of your room) to yourself at the hotel fax number. Most hotels do not charge for incoming faxes, and these days hotels that cater to the business traveler often have top-quality, plain-paper fax machines. (Many such hotels also have fax machines in guest rooms; so, if you're lucky enough to snatch one of these rooms, you can use the same strategy without involving anyone from the lobby.)

Voilà! Shortly after sending a fax to yourself, the message light on your phone starts blinking. If you're like some of us who work into the wee hours of the morning, this is a particularly convenient way to get your documents printed in the middle of the night. (By the way, if you need multiple copies, send multiple faxes!) And if you happen to be staying at an especially service-oriented hotel, someone from the reception desk will gladly hand-deliver your printed document to your room. When you're frantically preparing for an important meeting at 8 A.M. or you're desperate to see the printed layout of a report you need to e-mail before going to sleep, receiving faxes in your hotel room at 2 A.M. will seem like a special treat. Trust me, it can be better than 24-hour room service!

TIP²

As most users of standard remote technology are aware, the capabilities of our equipment (hardware and software) far exceed our typical access of features and capabilities. (It's somewhat analogous to the vast capacities of the human brain that remain untapped.)

You can probably easily identify any number of capabilities of your equipment that, if you took the time to activate these capabilities, could make your life simpler or more efficient. So, find at least two such capabilities (program the speed dials on your phone or fax, learn how to send/receive faxes from your computer, install software you've been meaning to install, learn how to use the scanning feature on your fax machine, commit to using one of the database management programs you have access to, etc.).

Select the two capabilities that could be most advantageous to your work, and begin to let those capabilities work for you.

TRANSFER IT PROMPTLY TO IMPROVE PERFORMANCE

99 Protect Your Equipment (and Your Livelihood)

After hours of research, comparison shopping, poring over manuals, installing equipment, talking with help-desk technicians, finding and installing lights, rearranging furniture, working with the telephone company, and coordinating with the electrician, you will have amassed a significant investment in capital equipment and personal energy to create the optimal office solution for your telecommuting needs. And it's an investment you need to protect from loss, damage, and down-time, since your ability to work productively undoubtedly depends on the continued availability of your technology tools and other valuable equipment and resources. Beyond the inconvenience and impact on your business, the cost of replacement may be quite significant for many of the items in your office. With this in mind, be proactive about protecting your investments, and don't be lulled into complacency or avoidance with "I don't have time to think about it" or "It could never happen to me" thinking. Go beyond thinking about it and do some planning, followed by some quick action, on the following:

- *Warranties*. Always investigate the warranty options with your equipment purchases. In cases where the equipment is critical (such as your primary computer or the high-end color printer without which your output drastically diminishes), consider extended warranties that may include on-site service and/or equipment replacement within one business day.

- *Power supply*. All valuable equipment should operate on batteries, circuits, or power strips that guarantee surge protection.

- *Fire protection*. At a minimum, install fire and smoke alarms. Sprinklers may be cost-prohibitive, but you could consider a compromise with fire/smoke alarms connected to your security system (which automatically signals a fire alarm and gets emergency services rolling). Don't forget about fire *avoidance*: use of extension cords, overloading circuits, old wiring that you may be overworking, stacks of paper, use of portable heaters, etc. (Tip 17). Also, buy a fire extinguisher for your office, especially if you smoke or use flammable materials for your work.

- *Security*. Depending on the value of your business assets, the location of your office (in terms of visibility and access from the street), and the crime rate in your neighborhood, it may be advisable to install a security system in your office. Systems range from motion detectors that sound a local alarm to hard-wired motion and intrusion sensors that send a signal to a central security facility or directly to your local police. Don't forget the basic security measures you should take (whether or not you have an installed security system): lock doors and windows; use internal lights on timers and external lights activated by motion; and don't let mail, newspapers, and packages pile up at your door when you're away.

- *Insurance.* In the event that other protection measures fail, an act of God blows the roof off your house, or that wonderful old shade tree just outside your window falls through your office, it would be handy to have property insurance for the contents of your office. Your employer may be able to easily provide coverage against certain perils for the company-owned equipment in your home office. Otherwise, talk with your insurance agent regarding a rider on your homeowner's or renter's policy; most such policies will not cover business equipment and property without a special provision. The additional cost is likely to be worth the investment in light of the value you stand to lose in the event of any unexpected unpleasantness. (Don't forget to also investigate additional insurance coverage you may require for liability, especially if you have co-workers, clients, or subcontractors visiting your home office.)

TIP²

! Evaluate the security of your office and take immediate steps to retrofit locks on any doors or windows without adequate locks.

! Think about how your office (and your home) looks when you're away: Does it invite interest from potential intruders?

! Request a security audit by your local police department (often available at no expense) to get a professional and objective perspective.

! Consider investing in a security system to provide the level of protection you need.

100 So, Do You Really Need a Speakerphone in the Bathroom?

There was a cartoon published a few years ago that depicted the typical "wired" businessperson on vacation at the beach, completely tethered to all the equipment we thought would free us: telephone, computer, fax machine, printer, etc. Now, of course, cellular phones, PDAs, and computers are wireless, so you can still be technologically tethered on vacation, in your car, during time with your family, on airplanes, in your home, at social events, on the weekend, or just about anywhere (if you're not careful). How do you determine when technology threatens your work/life balance? For all the advantages we gain from the gizmology that makes telecommuting possible, there are some downsides you should be aware of and manage proactively.

What are the warning signs that you may be overdoing the use of technology in your work and your life? The key indicator is you. Here are some warning flags to look for:

- You're in a restaurant or other public place and a cell phone or pager starts signaling. It's not unusual for several people to begin checking their pockets or briefcases to see whether the signal is coming from their equipment. If you're scrambling to determine *which* of your multiple pieces of wireless technology it is, you're probably packing too much technology for one person.

- You have a growing awareness of knots in your stomach or barely perceptible waves of anxiety activated by sounds of your technology interrupting you when you're supposed to be away from work, relaxing, spending time with friends or family, etc. While occasional interference (during the closing of the fiscal year or the critical phase of a major project, for example) might be expected, the persistent and increasing level of interruptions could demotivate, discourage, or eventually depress you.

- If you find yourself yearning for the days when no one could communicate with you while you were on board an airplane, train, or ship; commuting to work; on vacation; shopping; at a sporting event; or enjoying an evening of Monopoly with your kids, you may need to re-establish some new boundaries that are "technology proof." For example, turn off the pager and cell phone at the end of the work day, do not carry your PDA to the PTA meeting, and have at least one vacation a year that's "computer-free."

Your family or friends might wave a few warning flags of their own. If you're a highly motivated, goal-focused, and driven type of person, you may just love having so much instant connection with your work, your clients, your co-workers, and your income opportunities. However, it may be "overload" for those who love and care about you and a source of stress and anger for them. If the intrusion of technology in your life becomes detrimental to your personal relationships, it's time to take note, reevaluate your priorities and readjust your behavior.

On the other hand, if technology will truly help you, go for it! Case in point: If you need a speakerphone in the bathroom, don't hesitate to install one! Yes, I have one. It's a vestige of my last corporate telecommuting stint when a member of my team persisted (in spite of requests and coaching to the contrary) in leaving inordinately long and detailed voice mail messages. I finally realized that: (1) this person's behavior was not likely to change without some type of personality change; (2) I wasn't in the personality counseling business and needed the contributions of this team member; (3) it was up to me to find a way to work around this obstacle. The speakerphone in my bathroom was the solution. After installing it, I productively completed my teeth/hair/make-up routine each morning to the accompaniment of those lengthy voice mail messages that were out of my in-box by the time I reached my office. Of course, I don't have speakerphones in every bathroom in my house, nor is it a technology tool necessary for most people under most circumstances.

All of this is very much a delicate balance in that your comfort with and acceptance of technology as an integral part of your work life is critical to your success as a telecommuter. And unless you completely compartmentalize your life (not terribly feasible anyway), technology really becomes part of your entire life. By all means, use whatever technology makes your life simpler, more integrated, more efficient, or more fun. Just be certain those technological tools that enable your success as a telecommuter do not also compromise your balance, peace of mind, sense of satisfaction or primary relationships.

TIP²

Are you using technology to its best advantage in your life? Are there new or upgraded tools you can acquire (e.g., integrated digital phone/pager, PDA) that will simplify your life, lighten your load when you're away from the office, or save you precious time?

If you haven't done so for a while, browse through some catalogs, magazines, Web sites, or retail outlets that cater to the technological needs of telecommuters, virtual offices, or road warriors. Assess your current technology needs and consider how new technology tools (or new ways of using your existing tools) can help you.

TRANSFER IT PROMPTLY TO IMPROVE PERFORMANCE

101 Make Telecommuting Work Well for You

When I reflect on why telecommuting has been so valuable to me— to my happiness, sense of balance, emotional and psychological well- being—several thoughts come to mind. Initially, though, I'm struck by the reminiscent feeling of leaving my house early in the morning before the sun crested the horizon, knowing I wouldn't return to my little sanctum of serenity until it was dark again. In those days BT (before telecommuting), I didn't consciously yearn to:

- Eliminate the commute (it's something you just get used to and accept);

- Spend more time in my home, which seemed (when office days were combined with my travel days) more like a hotel than a place to nurture a full, balanced, enriched and more multidi- mensional life.

- Give up wearing the corporate "look" (in spite of the expense and hassle of it all).

No, it was more subtle than that. Slowly I began to tire of the utter inefficiency of:

- My morning routine (hair, make-up, suit/dress, jewelry).
- A fairly nonproductive commute time (although I made the best of it as I honed my mobile multi-tasking skills!).
- LONG days in the office that seemed consistent primarily for the excessive number of meetings, interruptions and working lunches that left minimal time for handling the growing mounds of mail, messages, and assignments that required focused time.

At some indiscernible point, I moved from (1) growing dissatisfaction with the way work was integrated into my life (or, more pointedly, the way work consumed my life), to (2) an awareness that something needed to change, to (3) a determination to make a change and to craft a life that more appropriately integrated and balanced work with other priorities. This all led to my conviction that working from home was the solution, and I moved in a direction that was more open to possibilities and opportunities for telecommuting.

Was it easy? No! (Was it worth it? ABSOLUTELY!!) I learned how to make telecommuting work for me through trial and error. I've also learned that you don't have to make the mistakes and false starts I did. Many of the secrets of telecommuting success can be shared, and that led to the reason for this book. You, too, can find ways to work from home successfully IF you have a determination to achieve telecommuting success *and* a plan to ensure your effectiveness.

I believe the determination it takes emanates from a clear focus on what's important in your life (Tip 2), as well as a clear understanding of how to be successful in your job (Tip 3). Other skills, tools, systems, processes and procedures (Tips 4–100) enable your ability to support your determination and vision. The combination of all of these is the key to your success as a telecommuter!

A small sign sits on the windowsill next to my desk. It has traveled with me through many jobs and has always been visible from the desk of any office I've occupied. My little sign summarizes my belief about your potential success as a telecommuter if you apply the knowledge available to you:

ALL THINGS ARE POSSIBLE

TIP²

Use the following TELECOMMUTING IMPLEMENTATION GUIDE according to your individual needs and circumstances. Remember that few great things ever occur without a plan!

If you are:	**Use the Telecommuting Implementation Guide as a:**
• Thinking about becoming a telecommuter.	• Tool to help you assess the steps you'll need to take and resources you'll need to become an effective telecommuter.
• Ready to begin telecommuting.	• Start-up guide to "jump start" your telecommuting success.
• Already a telecommuter.	• Template by which you can evaluate your current telecommuting practices and identify any areas of concern, need or opportunity for improvement.

TRANSFER IT PROMPTLY TO IMPROVE PERFORMANCE

Telecommuting Implementation Guide

This guide is designed to help you achieve telecommuting efficiency and effectiveness. It will assist you in identifying factors that contribute to your success as a telecommuter and in designing a plan to accelerate your move from telecommuting novice to being a high-performing, competent, and confident telecommuter. If you have already begun telecommuting, this guide will help you fine-tune your ability to become more focused, effective, efficient, prosperous, and satisfied as a telecommuter.

☑ Your Telecommuting Success Potential

⇨ Use the Telecommuter Self-Assessment Checklist (Tip 1) to identify any potential barriers, areas of concern, or possible difficulties for you as a telecommuter (Personal Traits/Preferences) or in connection with your job (Job Appropriateness).

⇨ Evaluate the impact any obstacles may have on your effectiveness and satisfaction as a telecommuter.

⇨ Take measures to eliminate barriers and take action to ensure that all success factors are thoroughly addressed.

☑ The Telecommuting Agreement

Whether you are persuading your employer to support your telecommuting arrangement (Appendix A) or you're part of a corporate initiative that's mandated the telecommuting program, agreements between you and your employer should be thoroughly discussed and clearly documented. Issues that should be covered by the agreement include:

⇨ **Terms & Conditions**

+ Nature and scope of the telecommuting arrangement.
+ Limitations and rights associated with the telecommuting arrangement.
+ Clarification of the employee's job function, title, compensation and benefits, as well as a statement specifying that these are not altered by the telecommuting arrangement.
+ Costs (e.g., telephone installation and service, equipment, Internet/cable connection fees, post office box, or mailbox fees, etc.) the employer will and will not reimburse in connection with telecommuting.
+ Insurance coverage the employer will provide, as well as any coverage the employee is expected to purchase.
+ Rights and limitations of workers' compensation coverage for accidents in the home office.
+ On-site office inspections the employer will have the right to make.

⇨ **Employee Expectations**

+ The employee's specific and measurable accountabilities, including measurement methods and projected review dates.
+ Number of days the employee will telecommute.
+ Specific days or number of days in an established time-frame that the employee will be in the main office or in a satellite office.
+ Hours of availability the employee will maintain in the off-site office.
+ Frequency with which the employee will be in contact with the office via e-mail, voice mail, etc.
+ Any minimum standards regarding office configuration, safety, and security features.

⇨ **Communication Plans**

+ Alternative methods by which the employee will maintain communication with co-workers and others.
+ Frequency with which the employee and supervisor will talk, meet face-to-face, review results.

* Type and frequency of meetings the employee will attend as a remote or on-site participant.
* The plan for communicating the telecommuting arrangement to and securing commitments of cooperation from co-workers and support teams.
* Projected timeframe and process for review of the telecommuting arrangement and for making any necessary adjustments to the agreement.

⇨ **Equipment**

* Specific equipment the employee will purchase, provide and maintain at his/her own expense.
* Specific equipment the employer will provide, service, and maintain, including how such equipment should be procured.
* Restrictions on the personal use of company equipment or supplies located in the employee's home office.
* Ownership rights the employer maintains over equipment, software, reference materials, supplies, etc. and how such property will be returned in the event of termination of employment.

☑ Your Family Agreements (Tips 31, 35, 42, 44, 47)

Meet with your family to discuss reasons for your telecommuting arrangement, the nature of your work and your need for their co-operation, flexibility, and support. Specifically, be sure to have clear agreements regarding the issues listed below. Also, discuss issues in a way that establishes openness in sharing feelings, asking for and responding to concerns, seeking input and suggestions, asking for agreement and commitment, and making a specific commitment to have follow-up discussions.

⇨ The reasons and need for telecommuting
⇨ Acceptance of the in-home office
⇨ Location of the office
⇨ Need for privacy and absence of distractions
⇨ Handling of childcare
⇨ Limitations on use of company equipment and materials
⇨ Support for the telecommuting arrangement

⇨ Acceptance of the telecommuter's presence in the home throughout the day

⇨ Justification and process for interruptions

⇨ Answering of phones

⇨ Process for handling disagreements and concerns

☑ Office location and layout (Tips 12, 13, 15, 16)

⇨ Consistent with zoning or lease limitations

⇨ Adequate space

⇨ Room to expand

⇨ Adequate storage

⇨ Separate from home area

⇨ Sufficient distance from distractions and noise

⇨ Comfortable and pleasant

⇨ Excellent lighting

⇨ Sufficient ventilation

⇨ Adequate number of electrical circuits

⇨ Layout to promote efficiency and smooth work flow

☑ Equipment, furniture, and supplies (Tips 83, 85)

Not all items listed below are applicable in every situation. Use this guide to select those tools and resources you need to support your job, your office, your efficiency, and your personal work style.

☑ Technology Resources (Tips 87, 88)

⇨ Computer, desktop

⇨ Monitor

⇨ Glare filter

⇨ Mouse or trackball

⇨ Port replicator/docking station

⇨ High-speed modem

⇨ Adapters (for car lighter or cell phone)

⇨ Document holder

⇨ Personal pager

⇨ Fax machine (dedicated or multi-purpose)

⇨ Computer, notebook
⇨ Keyboard
⇨ Printer(s)
⇨ Scanner
⇨ Zip drive
⇨ External disk or CD-rom drive
⇨ Surge protection/power strips
⇨ Copier
⇨ Personal digital assistant
⇨ Calculator

☑ Equipment—Miscellaneous (Tips 89, 92)

⇨ Telephones & accessories
⇨ Lamps and lights
⇨ Hole punch
⇨ Pencil sharpener
⇨ Disk and CD holders
⇨ Flashlight
⇨ White board or paper easel
⇨ Rolodex
⇨ Utility knife
⇨ Paper shredder
⇨ Headset
⇨ Microcassette or small recorder
⇨ Transcription machine
⇨ Label maker
⇨ Typewriter
⇨ Paper cutter
⇨ Letter opener
⇨ Postage scale or meter
⇨ Clocks
⇨ Rulers

☑ Furniture (Tips 88, 93)

⇨ Desk

⇨ Computer work station
⇨ Shelves
⇨ Storage cabinet
⇨ Carpeting
⇨ Trash cans
⇨ Chair
⇨ File cabinets
⇨ Bookcases
⇨ Printer/fax/copier stands
⇨ Chair/floor mats
⇨ Cork, bulletin, or white board

☑ Supplies (Tip 85)

⇨ Toner and ink cartridges
⇨ File folders and labels, varied colors
⇨ Labels (shipping, filing)
⇨ Pens, pencils, markers
⇨ Tape, various types with dispensers
⇨ Rubber bands
⇨ Paper weight
⇨ Trash cans
⇨ Paper towels/tissues
⇨ Spare batteries
⇨ Stamps
⇨ Paper (various sizes and colors)
⇨ Envelopes, varied sizes
⇨ Scissors
⇨ Staplers, staples, and staple remover
⇨ Paper and binder clips
⇨ Self-stick notes (various sizes and colors)
⇨ Rubber stamps
⇨ Desk accessories and organizers
⇨ Calendars
⇨ Binders/folders

Appendices

Appendix A

"Make a Case for Telecommuting" Guide

You may be interested in telecommuting and ready to experiment with it before your employer has given it much consideration. While this circumstance is not uncommon, you certainly can increase your odds of gaining approval for telecommuting by being uncommonly prepared in the way you propose and plan your telecommuting arrangement. Depending upon your company, your job, your boss, and the current state of business at your company, you may need to have several meetings with people from various departments, as well as numerous discussions with your boss.

Bear in mind, also, that while your boss may be very supportive, you may need to supply additional information for your boss to use in persuading other managers or executives to approve your proposal. This may involve meetings, presentations, and written (as well as rewritten!) proposals. To streamline and focus your effort, use the following guidelines for exploring and initiating an implementation of telecommuting for your job. (Consult the addendum to this Appendix for additional information on the telecommuting trend.)

1. Plan and prepare with corporate benefits in mind

Your "frame of reference" for your approach, rationale, and specific plans should be based on what's in the best interest of your job, your manager, your company, and your customers. Therefore, while many of your reasons for wanting to telecommute might be personal and relate to advantages you and your family will realize, it's critical that you focus on the numerous advantages telecommuting also offers your employer, such as:

- Increased productivity
- Lower real estate space costs

- Reduced equipment/furniture costs
- Reduced employee turnover
- Reduced absenteeism
- Increased customer satisfaction
- Improved morale
- Improved work/life balance
- Legislative compliance
- More recruitment options
- Results-oriented management
- Effective use of meetings
- Increased flexibility
- Increased employment of women
- Increased employment of disabled workers
- Reduced travel costs
- Access to part-time or retired employees
- Competitive advantages
- Access to additional labor pools to address skill shortages

Tailor the benefits you present to the specific needs of your employer, citing corporate initiatives and "hot buttons" that are addressed by telecommuting. Where possible, provide specific examples of projected cost savings, comparative advantages realized by similar organizations, or detailed examples of ways productivity measures will improve as a result of telecommuting for your job. If there are particular problems your company currently is facing (e.g., shortage of space) that telecommuting can impact immediately and directly, be sure to highlight these. At a minimum, you should be able to cite specific improvements in productivity that will result and translate these into a dollar amount your employer can expect to save. (Consult Appendix B for research resources available through various Web sites.)

2. Explain why you will be an effective telecommuter

Provide a list of personal traits for telecommuting success (Tip 1) and review how you meet the criteria. Explain in detail why you are a good candidate for telecommuting. You can include some of your personal reasons for wanting to telecommute, although your primary emphasis should remain on the business reasons and advantages telecommuting offers the business enterprise.

3. Explain how you will make telecommuting work
Describe in detail how you will handle your:

- Major job accountabilities
- Daily tasks
- Key co-worker relationships
- Interactions previously handled as face-to-face

Provide a detailed summary of your:

- Projected daily schedule
- Measurable results and methods to report achievement of goals on a routine basis
- Alternative methods for keeping in touch and maintaining your accessibility to co-workers, managers, vendors, and clients
- Support from other departments and functions from whom you've secured commitment (e.g., information systems/computer support, telecommunications, real estate, human resources/ personnel, marketing, accounting)
- Location and layout of the home office space you will use
- Plan for handling childcare, family care and other family-related issues
- Projected equipment needs (and estimated costs for equipment/supplies to be provided by your employer)

4. Suggest a telecommuting pilot
If your boss or others are not ready to "take the plunge" and approve your permanent transition to telecommuting, propose a telecommuting pilot to gather more information, uncover unexpected problems, and identify additional ways to enhance productivity. For example, you might suggest that you telecommute one day each week for two months. Be sure, however, to have the pilot details

clearly documented, as well as an agreement on the criteria for evaluating success of the pilot. Your pilot proposal should include any projected costs (e.g., phone line installation or phone expenses for use of your home phone line, purchase or loan of a notebook computer, etc.).

Bear in mind that any pilot program, while measures may be clearly established, may give you less than stellar results. While it may be appropriate for your employer not to make any major investments in equipment, systems, training, or communication, this also will negatively impact the pilot results. For example, remote access to your corporate network or server may be cumbersome and may negatively impact your projected productivity improvements. Consider these factors when evaluating pilot results and use them as instructive points in the proposed design for your proposed telecommuting plan.

At the conclusion of the telecommuting pilot, present the results by reviewing the established criteria and measurements, any obstacles or concerns, and any unexpected results. Revise your original proposal and plan to resubmit or re-present it with the inclusion of pilot results. If the pilot achieved acceptable results and/or affordable solutions to overcome obstacles can be proposed, make a formal request for approval of an expanded or permanent telecommuting arrangement.

Addendum to Appendix A

The Telecommuting Trend

As a telecommuter, you're part of one of the most significant and exciting trends impacting the workplace. A wide range of organizations are actively utilizing telecommuting as both an alternative and an enhancement to traditional approaches to conducting business. The number of people who telecommute continues to increase each year. Organizations, both large and small, throughout the United States employ more than 11 million telecommuters. Recent studies estimate there are now more than 50 million home-based workers, including full-time and part-time home-based business owners, as well as telecommuters.

What Is Telecommuting?

Telecommuting redefines the workplace to enable people to work from home or from other locations during a portion of the work week. There is a continuum of options available to individuals and organizations that want to realize the benefits of telecommuting. This range of options takes into consideration amounts of time spent working in an office, at home or other remote locations.

TELECOMMUTING CONTINUUM

Informal Telecommuting	Part-time Telecommuting	Hoteling	Telecenter	Telecenter/ Telecommute	Full-time Telecommuting

If you're an **informal telecommuter**, you may work at home occasionally (e.g., when you need to be there to meet a service provider, tend to a sick child, avoid a major traffic or weather obstacle, etc.). Also, many people routinely work at home in the evenings or on weekends just to "catch up" or keep on top of time-sensitive projects. The expanded use of voice mail, e-mail, laptop computers, and cellular phones has facilitated this dynamic (or this intrusion, as some might think). Nevertheless, there's an undeniable increase in work-related activity occurring in our homes during nonwork hours.

Part-time telecommuters blend their on-site work days with work-at-home days, usually telecommuting only a day every week or two. These arrangements can be structured to involve specific telecommute days (e.g., every other Friday) or can be variable, depending upon individual and organizational needs.

Your "on-site" time as a telecommuter can involve a range of options that may include work days in the corporate office, a field office, a client site, a vendor site, a conference room at an airport, or some other remote location. There may be a dedicated office space for you in the traditional workplace, such as your "cube" at corporate. However, with the increase in telecommuting and the imperative to curtail spiraling real estate costs, many organizations are opting to utilize **hoteling** or other alternative officing arrangements to support telecommuters. With hoteling, telecommuters have a temporary office available for their use while in the office. The range of services may include personalized phone extensions to which your calls are automatically transferred, personal files that are moved into your temporary office on the days you're scheduled to be there, and assistance from a "concierge" for scheduling and coordination of on-site support.

Some organization and branches of the federal government have established **telecenters**, which often serve as regional or suburban-based work hubs. These afford workers the opportunity to minimize commuting time to corporate offices while offering the advantages of shared facilities, team interaction opportunities, and less reliance on a home-based work arrangement. Some telecommuters combine their work-at-home days with on-site days at the telecenter, providing even greater flexibility by blending the **telecenter/telecommute** options.

Although the balance between on-site work days and home-based work days may find some telecommuters working primarily from home, **full-time telecommuting** is very rare and difficult. Few jobs are conducive to practically no on-site time or interaction opportunities with co-workers. In reality, full-time telecommuters are typically those for whom the home office is their *primary* work location (that is, where they typically do their work; receive mail, faxes, phone calls, and voice mail; participate in virtual meetings and, perhaps, some face-to-face meetings). These telecommuters, along with others who work from home less frequently, don't function in isolation. On-site meetings and face-to-face interactions are still a necessary part of work, and telecommuters are simply more selective about when such "live" interactions are essential. Telecommuters and the organizations with which they work take advantage of available technology to supplement face-to-face meetings with other creative ways to meet the needs of the organization, employees, and customers.

Who Telecommutes?

The types of job areas conducive to telecommuting are varied and continually expanding. While there are hundreds of corporate job titles that are applicable, the positions or job categories most typically involved in telecommuting include: computer professionals, writers, administrative support, customer service, writing/communications specialists, sales representatives, trainers, management, professional line staff, research analysts, and data processing staff.

Beyond identifying the right JOBS for telecommuting, successful telecommuting programs ensure that the right PEOPLE are selected. Those who successfully telecommute have a unique combination of motivation and skills that are critical to their success as telecommuters. Determining who the right people are and developing their skills for telecommuting are the key differentiators in a highly successful telecommuting program.

According to the experiences of numerous organizations, successful telecommuters typically possess the following characteristics, traits, and skills:

- Planning and organizing abilities
- Time management skills

- Independence (works successfully without close supervision)
- Low affiliation needs
- Strong communication skills (written and verbal)
- Supportive family/home environment
- Self-motivated
- Self-disciplined
- Strong performance record
- Technical ability/high job knowledge
- Strong work ethic
- Computer proficiency (hardware, software, peripherals)

In addition to fitting this typical profile, prospective telecommuters should think twice about telecommuting if they:

- Have high affiliation needs
- Must be in an "office" to be motivated to work
- Are easily distracted by household demands (tasks, family, etc.)
- Do not have a supportive/cooperative family situation
- Do not have reliable child care arrangements during work hours

Wherever there are telecommuters, there are usually telemanagers. Distance managing requires so many of the skills and abilities that are critical to the evolving role of manager/supervisor to leader/coach. If you are functioning as a telemanager, keep in mind the following characteristics, traits, and skills that will contribute to your effectiveness:

- Performance management based on *results*
- Effective interpersonal communication (face-to-face and via technology)
- Honor commitments (face-to-face or phone meetings)
- Effective coaching/feedback skills
- Relationships built on mutual trust
- Planning and organizing
- Openness to change
- Computer proficiency

- Ability to effectively telecommute or understand the basic criteria for successful telecommuting

Making Telecommuting Work

Telecommuting, supported by the phenomenal increase in availability of cost-effective technology, is a workplace alternative that is here to stay. The convergence of economic, legislative, social, and family imperatives will foster the expansion of telecommuting as a viable work option. Therefore, organizations that want to prosper and people who want to maintain their proficiency will learn how to make telecommuting work well.

Appendix B

Telecommuting Resource Guide

Inclusion of resources and information in this guide does not imply an endorsement by either the publisher or the author.

☑ Associations

American Telecommuting Association
www.knowledgetree.com/ata-tai.html
yourATA@aol.com
800.282.4968

Home Office Association of America
www.hoaa.com
HOAA@aol.com
800.809.4622
10 Gracie Station, Box 806
New York, NY 10028-0082

International Telework Assocation and Council
www.telecommute.org
TAC4DC@aol.com
202.547.6157
204 E. Street, N.E.
Washington, DC 20002

Canadian Telecommuting Association
www.Ivc.ca
info@ivc.ca
613.225.5588
52 Stonebriar Drive
Nepean, Ontario, Canada K2G 5X9

☑ Newsletters/Magazines

Home Office Computing
www.smalloffice.com

Home Office Connections
www.hoaa.com

Telecommuting
www.telecommuting.about.com

Telecommute
www.telecommutemagazine.com
info@telecommutemagazine.com

TeleTrends
www.telecommute.org/teletrends.htm

The Telecommuting Review
www.gilgordon.com

☑ Conferences

alt.office Conference & Exposition
www.altoffice.com
prusso@mfi.com
800.950.1314

International Telework Association & Council (ITAC) Conference
www.telecommute.org
800.942.4978

Telework America
www.telecommute.org/twa_overview.htm
TAC4DC@aol.com
202.547.6157

☑ On-line Resources and Web Sites

For telecommuters and home-based workers:

ALLearnatives®
www.allearnatives.com
info@allearnatives.com
724.934.9349

The Disability Connection
www.apple.com/education/k12/disability

Fleming LTD
www.mother.com/dfleming
dfleming@mother.com
530.756.6430

Gil Gordon Associates
www.gilgordon.com
gilgordon@compuserve.com
732.329.2266

JALA International, Inc.
www.jala.com
jala@ix.netcom.com
310.476.3703

June Langhoff's Telecommuting Resource Center
www.langhoff.com

Pacific Bell Telecommuting Guide
www.pacbell.com/products/business/general/telecommuting/tcguide/index.
html

Telecommuting Safety & Health Benefits Institute
www.orednet.org/venice/rick/telecommutesafe
rijohnso@orednet.org

Telecommuting Success, Inc.
www.telsuccess.com
info@telsuccess.com
303.660.8135

TELEWORKanalytics international, inc
www.teleworker.com
tai@teleworkers.com
888.353.9496

Working Solo, Inc.
www.workingsolo.com
office@workingsolo.com
914.255.7165

For road warriors:

efax.com www.efax.com

Mobile Computing www.mobilecomputing.com

Mobilis www.volksware.com/mobilis

Road Warrior International www.warrior.com

For telecommuting job seekers:

Telecommuting Jobs www.tjobs.com

Telejobs.net www.telejobs.net

The Mining Co. www.telecommuting.about.com/msub3.htm

☑ Office Supplies/Services

Kinko's www.kinkos.com 800.2KINKOS

Mailboxes Etc. www.mbe.com 800.789.4MBE

Office Depot www.officedepot.com 888.GO-DEPOT

Pitney Bowes www.pitneybowes.com/soho 800.5Pitney

Office Equipment Outlet www.oeo.com 800.553.2112

OfficeMax www.officemax.com 800.283.7674

Staples www.staples.com 800.3STAPLE

☑ Express/Shipping Services

Airborne Express www.airborne.com 800.AIRBORNE

Federal Express www.fedex.com 800.GoFedEx

U.S. Postal Service www.usps.gov

DHL Worldwide Express www.dhl.com 800.CALL-DHL

United Parcel Service www.ups.com 800.PICK-UPS

☑ Information Services

Federal government statistics www.fedstats.gov

Information Please www.infoplease.com

Virtual Reference Desk www.refdesk.com

Roget's Thesaurus www.thesaurus.com

Hoover's www.hoovers.com

OneLook Dictionaries www.onelook.com

Internet Service Providers www.thelist.com

☑ Additional Reading About Telecommuting and Home-based Work

Digital Nomad, by Tsugio Makimoto, et al. (John Wiley & Sons, 1997)

Flexible Work, by Edna Murphy (Prentice Hall, 1996)

Home but Not Alone: The Parents' Work-At-Home Handbook, by Katherine Murray (Jist Works, 1997)

Home Office Know-How, by Jeffery D. Zbar (Upstart Publishing, 1998)

The Home Office Solution: How to Work at Home & Have a Personal Life Too, by Alice Bredin, et al. (John Wiley & Sons, 1998)

The Joy of Working from Home, by Jeff Berner (Berrett-Koehler Publishers, Inc., 1994)

Managing Telework : Strategies for Managing the Virtual Workforce, by Jack M. Nilles (John Wiley & Sons, 1998)

An Organizational Guide to Telecommuting, by George M. Piskurich (American Society for Training & Development, 1998)

Organizing Your Home Office for Success, by Lisa A. Kanarek (Blakely Press, 1998)

Telecommute! Go to Work Without Leaving Home, by Lisa Shaw (John Wiley & Sons, 1996)

The Telecommuter's Advisor: Working in the Fast Lane, by June Langhoff (Aegis Publishing, 1996)

Telecommuting: A Manager's Guide to Flexible Work Arrangements, by Joel Kugelmass (Lexington Books, 1995)

Teleworking: In Brief, by Mike Johnson (Butterworth-Heinemann, 1997)

Tips for Your Home Office (Enhancing Your Life at Home), by Meredith Gould (Storey Books, 1998)

The Ultimate Home Office Survival Guide, by Sunny Baker, et al. (Peterson Guides, 1998)

Work-at-Home Balancing Act: The Professional Resource Guide for Managing Yourself, Your Work, by Sandy Anderson (Avon Books, 1998)

Working Smarter from Home: Your Day—Your Way, by Nancy J. Struck (Crisp Publications Inc., 1995)

Index

About the Author

Debra A. Dinnocenzo is a veteran telecommuting executive with nearly 10 years of firsthand experience as both a telecommuter and telemanager. Her involvement in remote work and distance learning has spanned 20 years and involved work with groundbreaking technologies such as the electronic blackboard to more sophisticated videoconference applications. Ms. Dinnocenzo has managed sales forces and marketing departments in both traditional corporate settings and as a telemanager. While telecommuting, she was senior vice president of marketing for Learning International, a worldwide sales performance and training company and a division of Times Mirror.

Her experience in telecommuting led Ms. Dinnocenzo to found ALLearnatives®, a learning and development firm specializing in tools and resources to improve the productivity of telecommuters, telemanagers, and other home-based workers. In 1997 she was awarded runner-up honors in the Home Sweet Home-Office Contest sponsored by *Sales & Marketing Management* magazine.

Ms. Dinnocenzo resides in Pittsburgh, Pennsylvania with her husband (who also is a telecommuter) and their daughter.

For more information about the services and capabilities of ALLearnatives®, please contact us:

Web site: www.TipsForTelecommuters.com
E-mail: info@allearnatives.com
Telephone: 724.934.9349
Fax: 724.934.9348
Address: ALLearnatives®
10592 Perry Highway, #201
Wexford, PA 15090 USA

How To Get (and Give) More Information

For additional information about telecommuting or for additional tips for telecommuters, please visit the Website:
www.TipsForTelecommuters.com.
Additional information is also available at the address and phone number below.

To order additional copies of this book, visit the Web site:
www.bkconnection.com.

If you would like to contribute to the next publication in the **Tips for Telecommuters** series, we would appreciate hearing from you. Please send:

- Your own telecommuting tips that have helped you be a successful telecommuter.

- Your best and worst experiences as a telecommuter.

- Suggestions for topics or tips you'd like to see in a future edition or publication for telecommuters.

Be sure to include your name, job, organization, and contact information so we can acknowledge your contribution. Here's how to reach us:

Web site:	www.TipsForTelecommuters.com
E-mail:	info@allearnatives.com
Telephone:	724.934.9349
Fax:	724.934.9348
Address:	ALLearnatives®
	10592 Perry Highway, #201
	Wexford, PA 15090 USA

Thanks!